TWISTED TRUE TALES FROM SCIENCE

MEDICAL MAYHEM

TWISTED TRUE TALES FROM SCIENCE

MEDICAL MAYHEM

STEPHANIE BEARCE

WITH ILLUSTRATIONS BY
ELIZA BOLLI

 Prufrock Press Inc.
Waco, Texas

Library of Congress Cataloging-in-Publication Data

Name: Bearce, Stephanie, author.
Title: Twisted true tales from science : medical mayhem / by Stephanie Bearce.
Other titles: Medical mayhem
Description: Waco, Texas : Prufrock Press, Inc., [2017] | Audience: Ages
  9-12. | Includes bibliographical references.
Identifiers: LCCN 2016040582 | ISBN 9781618215727 (pbk.)
Subjects: LCSH: Medicine--History--Juvenile literature. | Medical
  sciences--History--Juvenile literature.
Classification: LCC R133.5 .B43 2017 | DDC 610.9--dc23
LC record available at https://lccn.loc.gov/2016040582

Edited by Lacy Compton

Cover and layout design by Raquel Trevino
Illustrations by Eliza Bolli

ISBN-13: 978-1-61821-572-7

Printed in the United States of America.

At the time of this book's publication, all facts and figures cited are the most current available. All telephone numbers, addresses, and website URLs are accurate and active. All publications, organizations, websites, and other resources exist as described in the book, and all have been verified. The author and Prufrock Press Inc. make no warranty or guarantee concerning the information and materials given out by organizations or content found at websites, and we are not responsible for any changes that occur after this book's publication. If you find an error, please contact Prufrock Press Inc.

Prufrock Press Inc.
P.O. Box 8813
Waco, TX 76714-8813
Phone: (800) 998-2208
Fax: (800) 240-0333
http://www.prufrock.com

TABLE OF *Contents*

ANCIENT DAYS

MEDIEVAL MALADIES

MODERN MARVELS

ANCIENT DAYS

THE
DOCTOR
IS IN

DISEASE AND DEATH

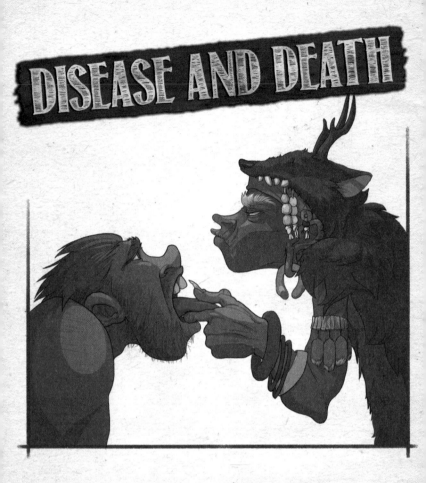

The boy lay in a cave on a pallet of furs. A woman crouched near him stroking his head and whispering a charm against evil. The shaman chanted and sprinkled dried leaves into a pot warming on the fire. He prayed as he stirred, asking evil spirits to leave the boy, and good spirits to bring him back to health.

When the tea was ready, the shaman poured it into a bowl. The woman lifted the boy's head and together they tried to pour the tea into his mouth, but they couldn't open the boy's jaw. The muscles were clenched so tight that the shaman couldn't pry his mouth open. Suddenly the boy began flailing. Legs kicked and arms jerked. The boy's back arched and collapsed. Then he was still.

The shaman backed away. Demons. The boy was possessed. There was no way to save him. The shaman chanted and backed out of the shelter. The woman wailed in grief and the boy's body began jerking and writhing again. Within a few hours, the boy would be dead. And his body would have to be burned to get rid of the evil.

It sounds like the scene in a horror movie, but this was medicine in prehistoric days. Sickness was a mystery. No one understood why a person was fine one day and throwing up the next. Why could a child be playing in the morning and then a few hours later have fevers and convulsions? And why did one person get sick and die while another lived? For prehistoric people, the only explanation seemed to be invasion by evil spirits. The shaman did what he or she could with plants, charms, and prayers, and sometimes it seemed to work. The person got better. The shaman would remember that cure and use it the next time a person in the village was infected. But modern medicine was centuries away.

The notion that tiny organisms living in soil, air, and water could make a person sick seemed more unbelievable than the idea of evil spirits. But without microscopes, X-rays, or ultrasound, prehistoric people had no idea what was going on inside the human body. Ancient healers experimented with different plants and found that some helped heal wounds and get rid of fevers. The healers were called whenever anyone in the village was sick. They became known known as shamans, kahunas, swnw ("sewnew"), sorcerers, mundunugu, witches, and priests. Eventually they were called doctors and physicians.

Some of the cures they discovered are still used today. Willow bark, chewed by people to relieve pain, is now used to make aspirin. The foxglove plant was often given to help when a person's heart was failing. Modern doctors use medicine from foxglove to treat heart disease. But other cures like pouring boiling oil on wounds and using dried snakeskin to cure blindness, are now understood to be bad medicine.

Some of the cures that people tried sound bizarre, like putting onions on the feet to stop a fever, or drinking urine to cure the plague. But in a world with no understanding of germs or bacteria, people were desperate to find something—any-

> The notion that tiny organisms living in soil, air, and water could make a person sick seemed more unbelievable than the idea of evil spirits. But without microscopes, x-rays, or ultrasound, prehistoric people had no idea what was going on inside the human body.

thing—to cure their illness. Without modern antibiotics and medicines, the average age of death was 45. One out of every three children died before they could celebrate their fifth birthday. Nearly 20% of pregnant women died from childbirth.

If a human survived to adulthood, he had to worry about catching a common cold. It could kill him. If the cold went into his lungs and turned into bronchitis or pneumonia, it was often a death sentence. There were no antibiotics to help cure these illnesses, so it was a matter of whether the body could survive the disease. Many didn't.

Getting hurt was just as dangerous. Simple cuts and scrapes could get infected, and without antiseptics, the injuries turned into gangrene and blood poisoning. The flesh literally rotted off the bone and the pain made victims scream in agony. Death seemed like relief.

And some, like the boy in the cave, got lockjaw from a bit of dirt in a cut. Lockjaw was caused by a disease called *tetanus*. It was a horrible death that triggered muscle spasms so severe that the jaw would lock shut and the whole body would jerk from the tightened muscles. The spasms were so violent that they could break the bones of the victim. Tetanus sufferers died writhing in pain and fever with no medicines to help.

Illness and disease were worldwide. In what would become modern-day China, Egypt, Turkey, Japan, and Italy, men and women struggled to figure out ways to help the sick and dying. They experimented on themselves, on sick neighbors and friends. When they found something that helped, they shared their knowledge with other healers.

It took thousands of years of trial and error, failure and success to develop the modern medicine humans use today. But now doctors are able to prevent diseases with vaccinations, cure infections with antibiotics, and perform surgery to help heal internal organs. There is still much to learn, but as long as humans keep getting sick, healers will continue to search for cures.

CAVEMAN CURES

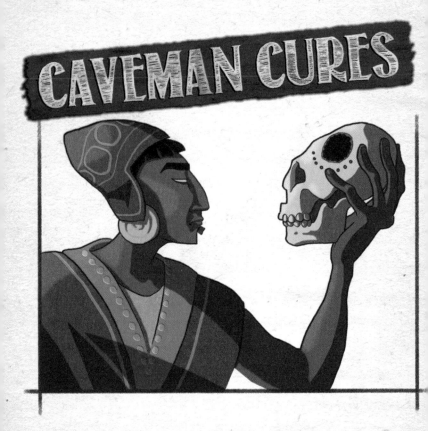

Surgery requires a sterile operating room, sharp steel scalpels, and doctors in surgical masks. At least that's the modern version of surgery. But if a prehistoric man in Peru got clonked on the head with a rock, chances are he might have had surgery, too. But instead of a scalpel, there was a rock drill, and instead of a licensed doctor, there was a medicine man or woman. And sterilization had not been discovered.

Trepanation, or skull surgery, has been around

since 6500 BC. Archaeologists have found evidence around the world of prehistoric skulls that had holes drilled in them and pieces of bone removed. What's even more amazing is that there is evidence of the skull bones *healing*. That means the patient survived the surgery with the rock drill and lived to tell the tale. Some skulls show that trepanation was done more than once to the same person.

Archaeologists believe that trepanation or skull drilling was used for a variety of reasons. Head injuries were common because hunting and warfare involved swinging clubs and throwing rocks. A medicine man would cut into the head at the site of the injury, scrape away the hair and skin, and drill through the bone to drain out blood from the head injury. This type of treatment is still done by doctors today to treat severe head trauma (though with real surgical tools!). Evidence of ancient trepanation surgeries has been found around the world from Africa to Asia to the Americas.

Surgery requires a sterile operating room, sharp steel scalpels, and doctors in surgical masks. At least that's the modern version of surgery. But if a prehistoric man in Peru got clonked on the head with a rock, chances are he might have had surgery, too.

But not all trepanation was done because of a blow to the head. Trepanation was also used to cure migraine headaches, epileptic seizures, and to get rid of evil spirits. Prehistoric people believed that by drilling a hole in the head, it allowed the evil spirits to leave the body and the patient would be cured. If he or she survived the surgery, the patient was given the piece of skull to keep. It was believed that the piece of bone would ward off any new evil spirits and keep away headaches and seizures.

Trepanning didn't die out with the cavemen. Doctors in 1500s Europe used drills to open up the skulls of their patients hoping to cure mental health problems and headaches. Prince Philip of Orange had his skull drilled into 17 times. His physician was sure this was the way to cure headaches. There is no report of whether or not it worked, but the prince did live to be 63 years old.

Most evidence found by archaeologists shows that while some people did survive having holes drilled in their skulls, many died. What is surprising about the studies is that the skulls from South American Mayan cultures show a much greater survival rate than those in European medieval times. The difference, perhaps? The Mayan doctors developed such sophisticated surgical skills that they made silver or gold plates to cover the holes drilled into the head. The bone then healed around the plates.

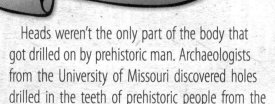

JUST SAY "AHHH"

Heads weren't the only part of the body that got drilled on by prehistoric man. Archaeologists from the University of Missouri discovered holes drilled in the teeth of prehistoric people from the area that is now Pakistan.

The holes were too perfectly round to have been made by decay. When scientists examined them under a microscope they saw evidence that the holes had been ground out by stone drills. Scientists believe that the holes were probably packed with medicinal herbs to relieve the pain of toothache. Believe it or not, people have been avoiding dentists since the days of the caveman.

PHARAOH'S FIX

Getting sick in Ancient Egypt was no fun. It meant being slathered in fat from dead cats and eating mixtures of herbs and animal dung. But during that time period, Egyptians had the best doctors in the world.

Because the Egyptians practiced mummification, they understood there were important organs inside the body. They knew about the heart, stomach, and digestive tract. Most other cultures had no idea what function organs had because they did not dissect or open human cadavers to look inside. It was considered evil to cut open a dead body, and because of that they were not able to learn about internal organs.

Egyptians were constantly studying the human body and had special schools to teach doctors about cures and medicines. They knew that scorpion stings and snakebites caused poisons to go into the body. They also understood how to set a broken bone and how to stitch deep cuts.

But the Ancient Egyptians did not understand anything about germs. They considered sickness to be a curse from the gods, and remedies included magic spells and potions. They wore small pieces of jewelry called amulets that were supposed to ward off evil spirits and protect them from illness.

The spells and amulets didn't provide any physical cures, but they may have helped people psychologically

> Egyptians were constantly studying the human body and had special schools to teach doctors about cures and medicines. They knew that scorpion stings and snakebites caused poisons to go into the body.

by having a placebo effect. This is when someone believes something will make them better so much that it actually seems to make them better. Modern doctors have studied the placebo effect by giving sick people fake medicine and have documented the fact that the sick person gets better. It shows the power of positive thinking—which may have helped some of the Egyptians.

Garlic and onions were believed to be important for good health, so ancient Egyptians ate them by the basketful. Fresh garlic was mashed and mixed with vinegar and used as a mouthwash. Any Egyptian who caught a cold rubbed his or her chest with mashed garlic and drank a garlic juice mixture to get rid of bronchitis.

Not all medicines were as pleasant as chugging garlic. Kids living in Ancient Egypt probably never complained about a toothache because nobody wanted to eat mouse paste. Yes, that's paste made from a dead mouse—a dead and festering mouse, as a matter of fact. Just

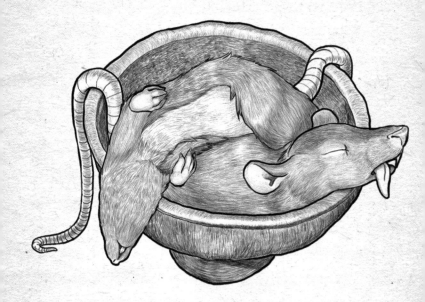

mash it up and mix it into a paste, then put it on the aching tooth. It's not a cure recommended by modern dentists, but many Egyptians were desperate. The sand from the desert got into almost all the food and ground down their teeth.

Of course, the cure for eye infections wasn't very fun either. Doctors recommended rubbing animal dung in the eyes (yes, that's right—poop). Waste from pigs, donkeys, lizards, and birds was used to cure cuts, scrapes, and rashes. The Egyptian physicians were trying to make the wound secrete a nice green pus. Of course, modern science tells us that pus is a sign of infection, but the Egyptian doctors thought it meant ridding the body of disease.

Needless to say, the average life span of a person in Ancient Egypt was not very long. Most people died when they were in their forties. A 20-year-old was considered middle-aged. And Egyptian medicine was still considered more advanced than that of the rest of the world.

THE BALDNESS CURE

Hair was in style during the days of the pharaohs. Baldness was just not cool. Doctors had several cures that people could try to get the peach fuzz growing. Most of the cures involved rubbing the fat of a dead animal on the head. Bald people were urged to try a mix of hippopotamus, crocodile, tomcat, snake, and ibex fat. If that didn't work, they could catch and skin a porcupine, boil the porcupine hair, and put it on their head for 4 days. Finally, if all else failed, they were told to take the leg of a female greyhound, sauté it in oil with the hoof of a donkey, and put *that* on the bald spot. If none of those worked, well—time for wig shopping!

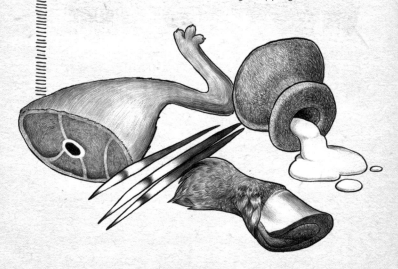

EAT YOUR DIRT

rown-ups probably tell you to "Drink your milk" and "Eat your vegetables," but have you ever heard someone say, "Eat your dirt?" Ancient Roman and Greek doctors advised their patients with stomach ailments to eat dirt to cure their problems.

A person suffering from ulcers or sores in the mouth was told to put dirt on them—or more accurately, cover them with red clay. Clay was also used to help stop ongoing stomachaches and pains (most likely caused by ulcers or acid reflux).

The clay was sometimes put into a porridge-like cereal called *alica*. The famous Roman physician Pliny the Elder wrote that when red clay was used as a drug it had a soothing effect. He recommended not just eating it, but using it as an enema to stop constipation.

> A person suffering from ulcers or sores in the mouth was told to put dirt on it—or more accurately, cover it with red clay. Clay was also used to help stop ongoing stomachaches and pains.

It was also eaten by pregnant women who seemed to crave the taste of clay. Midwives believed that small doses of clay could help women get over morning sickness. If the pregnant woman kept craving dirt, the remedy was to eat beans cooked with sugar.

Throughout history there are records of people from many parts of the world eating dirt and clay. Explorers from the 1800s wrote descriptions of South American members of the Otomacs tribe who included dirt in their regular diet. And eating clay was also considered normal and healthy for many tribes in Africa.

Today eating dirt or earth is called *geophagia* and has been documented around the world. Some doctors believe it is related to an eating disorder called *pica* where people eat all sorts of things that are not food (like paper, rocks, or cardboard).

But other scientists believe that eating dirt is a way people have adapted to lack of minerals in their diet. For instance, if a person did not have enough iron or calcium in her system, she may have bene-fitted from eating red clay that was rich in iron mineral or white soil rich in calcium.

Scientists also recognize that clay has binding properties that help absorb poisons. Native Americans used dirt or clay as a seasoning when cooking acorns and were able to eat them without getting sick. And modern medicines like Kaopectate and Pepto-Bismol use minerals from dirt to treat diarrhea and other digestive issues. So eating dirt might be good for you!

AN UNCOMMON CURE

Many cultures from Africa to Asia have old cures that involve smearing or rubbing animal dung or poop on an injury. One old cure for burns was to take the dung from a calf and burn it. Then place the ashes on the burn and leave it overnight.

For a cough, it was recommended to put cow poop in water and boil it. Once it cooled, the patient should gargle with the poop solution three times a day. It would either cure the cough or the patient would stop complaining about it.

Sheep poop stored in a tobacco pouch and hung around the neck was supposed to cure children of the croup. But tea made out of rabbit dung was what would get rid of a fever. Today, it is not advised that anyone consume animal dung for health or fun.

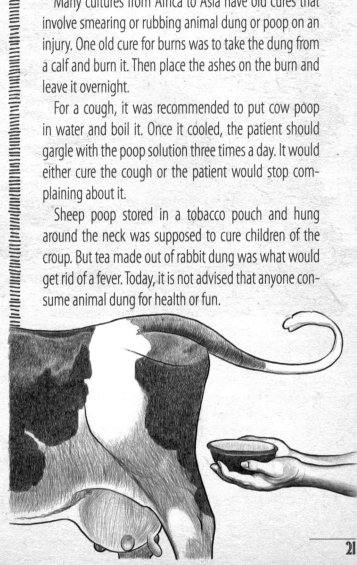

TRY TOBACCO

When Columbus sailed to the shores of the Americas in 1492, his crew members were the first Europeans to visit the Americas, but they certainly weren't the first to discover the continents. North and South America had thriving populations who had established trade routes, governments, and medicines. But because the Native Americans dressed differently and didn't have the same technology, the Spanish explorers believed they were an inferior culture. The Spanish missed out on the opportunity to learn a great deal about healing plants and medicines from the Native Americans.

The two plants that were most important to Native American medicine were tobacco and sage. The Spanish saw the Native Americans smoking tobacco for their religious ceremonies and quickly tested out the plant themselves. They were hooked. Literally. The nicotine gave the smoker a pleasant calming effect, but it was also quite addictive.

Native Americans knew about this and while some of them were addicted to tobacco, for many it was only smoked as a part of religious ceremonies. Tobacco was usually used as a medicine. Ground up and made into a poultice (a damp dressing), it was used to relieve the pain of earaches and toothaches. It was applied directly to the gum or ear and

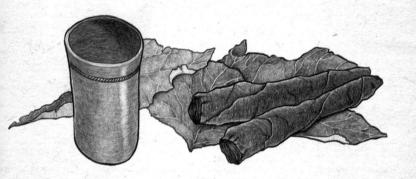

numbed the pain. Today, scientists are investigating how to extract the numbing properties from tobacco for possible use in modern medicine.

Native Americans also used tobacco poultices to help with insect stings and snakebites. Once the poison was sucked out of the snakebite, the poultice was applied and it helped reduce the swelling and inflammation. It worked just as well for wasp and bee stings.

Tobacco was also used as a toothpaste. Dried and ground into a powder, it was rubbed on the teeth for cleaning, and is still used as a method for teeth cleaning in India today.

Although tobacco has been known for the health problems it causes, scientists and doctors today are exploring some of the ways it can be used as a medicine to help those who suffer from problems like ADHD/ADD, schizophrenia, and Alzheimer's.

Sage is an herb that is frequently used in cooking. Most cooks add sage to the dressing for their Thanksgiving turkey. The Native Americans burned

Tobacco was also used as a toothpaste. Dried and ground into a powder, it was rubbed on the teeth for cleaning, and is still used as a method for teeth cleaning in India today.

sage in ritual ceremonies. The smoke was used to cleanse and purify the body and mind. Sage was also made into tea and was gargled to help soothe a sore throat. It was also used in bathing and washing hair to help keep the scalp and skin clean and fresh. Sage juice was said to help remove warts and reduce tumors.

Now, scientists are conducting research to see if sage can be used to help in the treatment of Alzheimer's disease, diabetes, and cholesterol. If the invading Europeans had taken the time, they could have learned some valuable medical lessons from the Native Americans.

ON PINS AND NEEDLES

The Chinese man was wealthy—extremely wealthy for a person living in 300 CE. He had a home with fine paintings and wore robes of beautifully dyed cloth. He had servants to care for his every need, but what he didn't have was health.

As was the custom in ancient China, his family and servants checked his urine and bowel movements every day. They looked to see if the urine

was cloudy, if the stool was a strange green or red color. They also looked at his tongue. For health, it should be bright red, not splotchy or gray. After days of examinations and doses of herbal teas, the family decided it was time to call in the physician. Something must be blocking the wealthy man's *qi* (life energy or blood flow) and medical help was needed.

When the doctor arrived, he spent a great deal of time feeling the man's pulse and reexamining the wealthy man's stool and urine. He talked to the wealthy man about his symptoms. Did he suffer pains in his back, stomach, or groin? After a thorough examination, the doctor made a diagnosis. The *qi* was definitely blocked. If it was not opened up to flow freely, the man would stay sick and have a slow, lingering death. The prescription was acupuncture and moxibustion.

> When the doctor arrived, he spent a great deal of time feeling the man's pulse and re-examining the wealthy man's stool and urine.

The doctor pulled out a set of finely sharpened steel needles. These were to be inserted into the wealthy man's body in several important areas to release the blockage of *qi*. The wealthy man lay down on his couch and the doctor pushed the needles into his skin and left them there. It would take a while to open up the channels and get the *qi* flowing.

Then the doctor prepared the mugwort for burning. The dried plant was finely ground and piled in a small cone on the man's back. A needle was pushed through the cone of mugwort deep into the skin and the mugwort was lit on fire.

The physician was encouraging the *qi* to move with the heat from the smoldering mugwort. The healing properties of the mugwort would pull the sickness out of the wealthy man's body. It would also leave blisters and scars after the treatment.

Within a few weeks, the wealthy man would declare himself cured or his family would call for another treatment. The treatment would be repeated until there was success or death.

This traditional Chinese medicine (TCM) is still widely practiced today. Acupuncture is used to help relieve back pain, muscle spasms, joint conditions, and dental pain. Even Harvard Medical School recognizes the worth of acupuncture for the treatment of chronic pain and recommends that when physical therapy, ice, and exercise don't help, acupuncture can help in 50% of cases.

Moxibustion has also been proven to be helpful in turning breech babies. Breech is when the baby's head is the wrong direction for safe birth. But mugwort is not placed directly on the skin of the mother and there are no blisters or scars. Instead, a needle is heated by a stick of burning mugwort. This causes the baby to turn in the mother's womb and prepare for a safe birth.

Many countries like Australia, New Zealand, South Korea, and Vietnam have accepted TCM as an alternative to Western-style healthcare, with people visiting their acupuncture doctor for a variety of healthcare reasons. It seems that the ancient Chinese physicians may have had the right cure after all.

THE LEGEND OF THE HONEY MUMMY

One of the strangest stories told in Chinese medical documents is about the mellified man. According to legend, elderly men living in Arabia would volunteer to become actual medicine. These men, who were in their 70s and 80s, agreed to go on a diet of only honey. They ate honey, drank honey, and even bathed in honey. Of course, a steady diet of honey will result in death.

Once the men died, they were placed in a specially prepared stone coffin and then covered completely with honey. The coffin was dated and sealed for 100 years. When they opened the coffin a century later, the contents were broken into pieces and sold as medicine. The pieces of the honey mummy were placed on wounded arms, legs, and broken bones to heal them. A very small amount taken internally was said to cure the most severe sickness.

Mellified man was supposedly very expensive and only the very wealthy could afford the cure. Although the story was recorded by Chinese pharmacologist Li Shizhen in the 1500s, there has never been any archaeological evidence found of this practice. Maybe the patients ate all of the evidence.

HONEY IS QUEEN

Turns out the ancient physicians were right about honey—not that you should eat honey mummies for health, but that honey is a great medicine. Scientists have discovered that honey's antibacterial qualities make it good for treating wounds. Cuts and scrapes heal better when they are rubbed with honey. The honey keeps the wound moist so that it can heal without drying out and it keeps away germs. So keep some of that bee juice around—it's great medicine that tastes good, too!

Medical Practice

HEART PUMP

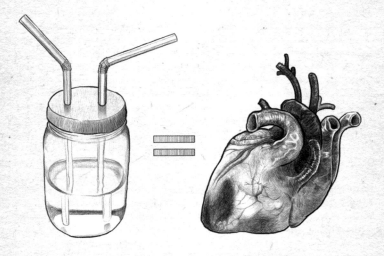

Understanding the heart has been the goal of physicians throughout the ages. Today, we have a better understanding of the heart than anyone did in ancient times. You can make a model of a pumping heart that would have made ancient doctors envious.

MATERIALS

- » Clean wide-mouth jar
- » Large balloon
- » Two flexible drinking straws
- » Wooden skewer
- » Scissors
- » Water
- » Tape
- » Large pan or sink

Fill the jar half full of water. Cut the neck of the balloon off right where it starts to widen into a bulb shape. Set the neck aside—you will use it later.

Stretch the balloon over the opening of the jar and pull it down as tight as you can. The flatter the surface, the better.

Carefully use the tip of the skewer to poke two holes in the surface of the balloon. Make them about an inch apart from each other and on opposite sides of the mouth of the jar. Stick the long part of a straw into each hole. The straws should fit securely so no air can get in around the straws.

Now you will need the neck of the balloon that you set aside earlier. Slide the uncut end of the neck onto one of the straws and tape it around the straw.

Set your pump in a large pan or in the sink so it will not get everything wet. Bend the straws downward. Gently press in the center of the stretched balloon and watch what happens to the jar.

You have created a simple pump that moved water from the jar through the straws and into the pan. The cut end of the balloon works as a valve to stop the water from going back down the straw. Your heart pumps blood out into your body through your arteries in a similar way.

SEE IT IN ACTION!

You can watch a short movie that demonstrates how to make this experiment at https://www.youtube.com/watch?v=pPjS52Ee9Jc

Here's a video on how the heart works: https://www.youtube.com/watch?v=ruM4Xxhx32U

Medical Practice

CHECK YOUR PUPILS

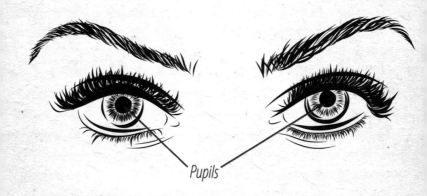

Pupils

Doctors have always known the eyes are important for understanding the body. In ancient times, physicians looked at the eyes to see if there were ailments in other parts of the body. Today, doctors check the pupils (black dot in the center) of a person's eyes if he or she gets hit on the head. The pupils should be the same size. If they are not, then the patient may have a concussion. The pupils should both react the same way to light. They should grow larger in a dark room and smaller in light.

Check out how the pupils work for yourself. All you need is a friend and a room with a light switch.

Dim the lights of the room. Get it as dark as you can. After a few minutes, look into the eyes of your partner and note the size of his or her pupils. Then turn the lights on. You should see the pupils shrink. This is the pupillary response. The pupil automatically closes to keep out excess light that could hurt the eye.

BLACK DEATH

1346

h. 08.00 ~ Yoga

h. 16.00 ~ Spread Black Death across Europe

h. 19.00 ~ Dinner with Mom

They called it Black Death because of the black pustules or buboes that popped out on the victim's neck, armpits, and groin. The egg-sized tumors oozed pus and sometimes grew to the size of an apple. They were accompanied by high fever and vomiting blood. It was a horrible disease that killed 80% of the people who caught it. And in the mid 1340s, it killed more than a third of the world's population. It was bubonic plague.

Nobody knows when the first plagues started—probably before humans knew how to write. The first recorded outbreak was in 541AD in Constantinople (modern-day Istanbul), but the most famous was a pandemic (worldwide epidemic) started in China in the 1330s.

China was famous for its beautiful silk fabrics and did a brisk trade with merchants from India and Europe. Traders went to China either by land on what was known as the "Silk Road" or by sea on ships. The plague probably spread both ways.

Historical reports tell of Chinese trade ships traveling to Sicily in October of 1347. When the ships docked in the Sicilian harbor, only a few of the sailors were alive. Most of the crew was dead. Those who were still living were covered in black, pus-filled

The egg-sized tumors oozed pus and sometimes grew to the size of an apple. They were accompanied by high fever and vomiting blood. It was a horrible disease that killed 80% of the people who caught it.

sores and delirious with fever. By the time the people of Sicily understood that the plague had sailed right to their doorstep, it was too late. The entire town became infected, and from there it spread to the mainland.

There was no cure for the plague in the 1300s. It requires strong antibiotics, and those would not be discovered for several centuries. Instead, desperate doctors and caregivers tried anything and everything to cure the disease.

Some doctors recommended lancing, or cutting open, the buboes to let the pus and blood drain out. Once the buboes were lanced, the doctor had three choices on how to proceed. He could let a dove drink from the blood, stick a feather in the open wound, or apply a poultice of tree resin, roots of white lilies, and human poop.

Other cures that people tried were drinking the pus from the lanced buboes, putting a live hen next to the sick person to draw out the impurities, and covering the sores with sprinklings of dried frog. None of these worked.

What doctors did not understand was that the disease

was first spread by the bites of fleas that lived on infected black rats. These rats lived in houses, on boats, in streets, in alleys, and in sewers. In a world without modern sewers or pest control, it was impossible to

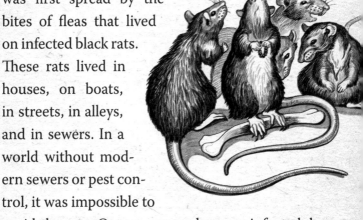

avoid the rats. Once a person became infected, he could pass the disease to another person through bodily fluids such as saliva, mucus, pus, or blood. Anyone who took care of the sick person became infected.

The plague spread terribly fast. A person might feel fine at breakfast and be dead the next morning. Most people died 2–5 days after the tumors appeared on their bodies.

There were so many people dying that they couldn't give them funerals. At night, the dead were taken from each home and laid out on the street. In the morning, teams of people came and collected the bodies on a cart and took them to a huge hole where they were buried in mass graves.

After a while, there weren't enough gravediggers left alive. Criminals were released from jail if they promised to serve as body collectors and gravediggers. Hundreds of people died every day and citizens were terrified. How could they save their families or themselves? Some decided that if they left the cities to go to the country they might escape the plague. But they carried the germs with them. No place was safe.

The outbreak of plague lasted for nearly 4 years, moving from China, India, and Europe on to the British Isles. It is estimated that it killed 25 million people in Europe and more than 75 million people worldwide. It took more than 150 years for the world population to recover from the Black Death. Outbreaks occurred until the 1600s, when cities began having more modern sanitation methods and doctors understood that quarantine could protect the general public.

There are still outbreaks of bubonic plague in the world today. The World Health Organization reports that there are between 1,000 to 3,000 new cases each year, but most are successfully treated with antibiotics.

PLAGUE SUIT

Some plague doctors wore a special protective suit when they were treating patients. It was supposed to protect the physician against the disease, but it also made him look like a monster from a horror film.

The suit included a coat made of heavy fabric that was coated with wax and a facemask that had glass eye openings and a cone-shaped nose that looked like the beak of a giant prehistoric bird. The nose cone was stuffed with straw and nice-smelling herbs like lemon balm, mint, and cloves. The straw and herbs were supposed to act as a filter for the doctors to keep away the bad air of the plague. They carried a long stick or cane so they could use it as a pointer and would not have to touch the plague patients. Unfortunately, the costume didn't work very well. Plague doctors got sick and died at the same rate of their patients.

A POX ON YOU!

In medieval times, there was no greater curse than to wish "a pox on you and your family." Smallpox was a horrible disease that covered the skin with pus-filled blisters and often killed its victims. Those who survived wore the scars for the rest of their lives. They had circular depressions covering their skin and disfiguring their faces. In severe cases, people lost parts of their lips and ears and the tips of their noses.

The first symptoms were fever, chills, headache, and backache. Then a rash covered the body and turned into pus-filled sores that made the skin feel like it was on fire. If the eyes were infected, they became cloudy and eventually all sight was lost. And most of the victims were children. It was a sickness that terrified parents because they knew that one in every three children who got smallpox died, and those who lived were scarred or blind.

> They had circular depressions covering their skin and disfiguring their faces. In severe cases, people lost parts of their lips and ears and the tips of their nose.

European doctors were helpless to stop the disease. They tried making pastes from plants and feeding patients herbal teas. They hung red curtains around the bed of the patient, hoping that the color red might take away the sickness. They even tried having the patient chew dried horse manure. Nothing helped. The one thing they did know was that people who recovered from smallpox never got the disease again even if they nursed a person covered with smallpox sores. Once a person had smallpox, he or she was immune.

Doctors in the East were centuries ahead of European medicine. In 1000 CE, Chinese doctors had already discovered how to inoculate people against smallpox. They collected scabs from small-pox patients, ground them up, and blew the powder into the noses of healthy children. It was blown up the right nostril for a boy and up the left nostril for a girl. The child would become ill, but it was a much milder case of smallpox without the horrible scars and with little chance of death.

In India and the Arabic world, pus was col-lected from the sores of sick people. The physician then made a small cut in the skin of the healthy person and rubbed the pus into the slit. Within a few days, the person would be recovering from a mild case of smallpox and was immune for the rest of his life.

It wasn't until the 1700s that the British learned about inoc-ulation. When Lord Montagu was named

Ambassador to the Ottoman Empire, his wife attended a smallpox party in Constantinople. The amazed Lady Montagu wrote back to her friends that while she was at the party an old woman pulled from her skirts a nutshell filled with smallpox pus. The old woman asked who wanted the treatment,

VACCINE FIT FOR A PRINCESS

In 1722, Princess Caroline of England wanted to have her daughters inoculated against smallpox, but she wanted to make sure that it was safe for the girls. So she promised six condemned felons that if they would test out the inoculation first they would

receive a reprieve of their sentence—if they didn't die from the inoculation. All six survived, but Princess Caroline wanted more proof. Next, she forced 12 children attending a charity school to be inoculated. When all of them survived and had only mild cases of small-pox, then she allowed the princesses to receive the treatment.

and adults and children held out their arms. She scratched them with a sharp needle and rubbed the pus into the wound.

Lady Montagu told her friends that the people suffered a mild form of the pox and were not scarred

> When Lord Montagu was named Ambassador to the Ottoman Empire, his wife attended a smallpox party in Constantinople. The amazed Lady Montagu wrote back to her friends that while she was at the party an old woman pulled from her skirts a nutshell filled with smallpox pus.

for life. Lady Montagu had contracted smallpox when she was 26 and her face was horribly scared. She was convinced this was the way to spare her own children from scars and possible death. In 1717, she had her 6-year-old son take the treatment. It was successful, and when she returned to England, she had well-known surgeon Charles Maitland inoculate her 3-year-old daughter.

News of this new procedure spread quickly and soon surgeons throughout the British Empire were busy inoculating patients and experimenting with ways to improve the technique. One such scientist was Edward Jenner, who began experimenting with the milder illness cowpox in the 1790s.

He had observed that milkmaids who had suffered cowpox were also immune to smallpox. He began using cowpox as an inoculation ingredient. His experiments were quite successful because the patients had an even lower death and illness rate. The public was frightened about using a virus that came from cows, however. Cartoonists published pictures showing people growing horns and hooves because they took the cowpox inoculation.

But Jenner's vaccine was so good at preventing illness that it was accepted by both the medical community and the general public. By 1814, more than 3 million people in Europe had been vaccinated

against smallpox. By the 1820s, smallpox vaccines were given around the world and Edward Jenner was recognized as the hero who stopped smallpox.

MAKEUP WAS MURDER

In the 1700s, makeup was in style for both men and women. Paintings of the nobility show pale white faces with bright red cheeks. They also show tall white powdered wigs and elaborate hairstyles.

The white face powder was popular because it helped hide the deep pit-like scars that many people had from smallpox. The powder was made from very finely flaked lead and made a nice thick covering that hid the scars. Unfortunately, the lead was highly poisonous and led to headaches, dizziness, and blindness. If the powder was accidentally ingested or eaten, it could lead to paralyzation or even death.

The red cheek rouge was not any better. Its ingredients included carmine, a lead-based pigment. The carmine was also used as lipstick, and it was next to impossible to avoid eating some of the lipstick. Many young ladies and gentlemen became gravely ill from the makeup they were using to hide their smallpox scars.

BLEEDING TO HEALTH?

George Washington spent the snowy December day on horseback inspecting his plantation. He marked some trees that he wanted to have cut, looked at fences and fields, and planned for the spring. At supper that night, he complained of a sore throat, but still read aloud to Martha from the newspaper. He went to bed refusing any medicine, saying, "You know I never take anything for a cold. Let it go as it came."

Early on the morning of Saturday, December 14, 1799, George Washington began having trouble breathing. Alarmed, Martha sent for Dr. James Craik, Washington's personal physician. The doctor immediately applied a preparation of dried beetles to his throat and cut open the veins on his arm. He drained 20 ounces of blood from Washington. When the president still had trouble breathing, the doctor drained 40 more ounces of blood. When he didn't show signs of improvement, the doctor gave him an enema to clean out his bowels. Then he called in two more doctors for assistance.

When Dr. Dick and Dr. Brown arrived, they all agreed that the only thing to do was to bleed the president again. This time they drained 32 ounces of blood from Washington. In a period of 10 hours, the doctors had drained out 3.75 liters of Washington's blood— more than half the total blood in his body. Washington died that night.

> The doctor immediately applied a preparation of dried beetles to his throat and cut open the veins on his arm.

Today, doctors would never drain a person of half his blood. Medical professionals know that too little blood causes hypotension and shock and often add blood through transfusions. But during

Washington's day, and for centuries before, doctors believed that removing blood was a good way to cure most diseases.

Bloodletting was done by the ancient Egyptians and Greeks, and in 200 CE, the famous physician Galen taught that the body was made up of four "humors"—blood, phlegm, yellow bile, and black bile. To be healthy, the humors all needed to be balanced. When they became unbalanced, it was believed that draining blood could put the humors back in balance. So doctors started the practice of bloodletting, or bleeding a patient to health.

Bloodletting was used to cure headaches, fevers, measles, mumps, rashes, stomach problems, smallpox, cancer, acne, scurvy, gangrene, and pneumonia. It was the first defense against any type of sickness and was even used to treat most forms of bleeding disorders and amputations.

The blood was taken several different ways. Venesection was the most common method, where a double-edged knife (lancet) was used to cut open a vein. The blood was drained into a bowl and measured. Some surgeons used blood-sucking worms called *leeches*. They laid the leeches on the person's body and let the leeches suck blood until they were full and fell off the patient. Another method was called *cupping*. Glass cups were heated and placed on the patient's skin until they caused blisters. The blisters were then sliced open and the blood drained.

Bloodletting was popular until the 1800s, when doctors like Pierre Louis began doing scientific studies on pneumonia patients. He compared those who had received bloodletting to those who had not and found a higher survival rate for those who got to keep their blood. More studies were done by scientists like Louis Pasteur, Robert Koch, and Rudolf Virchow. They all agreed that it was better for patients to have a full supply of blood in their body to help fight disease.

Today, there are a few diseases where doctors do remove blood from the body, such as hemochromatosis (too much iron in the body) and polycythemia (a problem with the volume of red blood cells), but both conditions are rare.

FREAKY FACT
LEECH CRAZE

Leeching was so popular that in the early 1800s there was actually a "leech craze" in England. Leech collectors would wade into murky waters where leeches lived and let the worms attach to their bare legs. They would then walk back on land and let the leeches suck blood until they were full and dropped off their legs. Then the leech collectors put them in jars and sold them to surgeons for a profit.

Unfortunately, the leech collectors often suffered from headaches because of the blood loss and often caught diseases from the contact with leeches and dirty water.

BARBER-SURGEONS

In the 1200s, a European barber was a very busy fellow. Not only did he cut hair and shave faces, but he also pulled teeth and performed amputations! During the Middle Ages, medical doctors did not perform surgeries. Cutting open the human body was considered extremely dangerous and was used as a last resort. Doctors did not want to be associated with the risky process of surgery and believed that bloody task was beneath them.

Instead, doctors worked as consultants with their patients, giving them advice on diet and dispensing herbal cures, poultices, and lotions. Monks and priests also provided herbal treatments and performed bloodletting to cleanse or purify the patient's system.

But in 1163, a church decree forbade monks and priests from performing the procedure of bloodletting. The public still believed that bloodletting was going to help them be healthy, so they turned to the professional who had a sharp set of knives. Barbers went into the business of bloodletting and continued the practice for more than 300 years.

Because barbers were skilled with knives, they were also called upon to accompany armies to war. With their knives and razors, they cleaned wounds,

removed gangrene, and, if necessary, amputated limbs. Royalty and wealthy citizens had their own barbers on staff. Common people consulted barbers for everything from rotten teeth to lice infections. Barbers were much cheaper than physicians, and during the Middle Ages most people could not afford to see a doctor. If someone was hurt, he or she would call the barber.

Barbers were both hairstylists and surgeons until 1800, when the formal Company of Surgeons was formed. Today, barbers are only licensed to cut hair.

BARBER POLE HISTORY

They are kind of rare today, but every now and then you catch a glimpse of a barber pole. It is a red, white, and blue pole or sign outside a barbershop. The colors on the barber pole date back to the Middle Ages, when a barber did much more than cut hair. The red on the pole indicates that the barber could be hired to do bloodletting with either leeches or a scalpel. The white represented the bandages used to stop the bloodletting, and the blue represents the veins.

Today, the red, white, and blue pole simply means that inside the store is a person who will cut your hair or give a shave. But a few hundred years ago, it meant a whole lot more.

NITPICKING

L ice. Creepy crawly tiny insects that hide in human hair and make the scalp itch. Just thinking about them makes most people scratch. Today, if a student has lice, she is sent home from school with instructions to get rid of the lice or she can't come back.

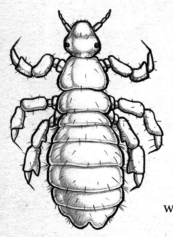

But lice have been a normal part of life for most of human history. Everybody had lice. Everybody itched and nobody really knew what to do about it. Bathing would have helped, but in medieval Europe bathing was difficult.

Water had to be drawn from a well or carried up from a river. Then the water had to be heated and poured into a wooden tub lined with sheets. It was hard work and not something that people did every day. When a family did prepare a bath, it was used by every person in the household. Once mom and dad were clean, each child was washed, all in the same water.

Men and women covered their unwashed hair with hats and scarves. They wore the same clothes for many days at a time. They shared sleeping mats and beds. All of these things combined to create the perfect breeding ground for lice.

Scratching and picking off lice or fleas was not to be done in public. When a lady's head itched, she would discreetly use a hairpin to scratch her head. Combs with fine teeth were used by both men and women to remove lice from their hair. Parents picked the lice out of children's hair, and nitpicking was a normal part of grooming. Bedding was sometimes washed in kerosene to get rid of lice, fleas, and bed bugs. But it was a constant battle because every person was a host to the creepy little critters.

When a family did prepare a bath, it was used by every person in the household. Once mom and dad were clean, each child was washed, all in the same water.

Not only were the lice itchy and gross, they also carried a nasty disease called *typhus*. It was sometimes called the "hazy" disease because when people fell sick with typhus, they went into a stupor, almost like a coma. The victims became feverish and had pains in their joints and muscles. Their bodies were covered in bright red rashes and their skin gave off a terrible stench.

Typhus thrived in places where there were lots of dirty bodies. Outbreaks happened in jails, on ships, and during wars. Napoleon's army suffered from "camp fever," or typhus, when they were trying to invade Russia in 1812. When Napoleon left France, he had an army of 600,000 men. By the time he reached Russia, his ranks had been reduced to only 90,000 men. Thousands of the soldiers had died of either typhus or dysentery. (Dysentery is a disease with severe diarrhea and a loss of blood.)

Soldiers, citizens, inmates, and sailors continued to suffer from lice and typhus until the early 1900s, when a scientist in North Africa, Charles Nicolle, proved that typhus was carried by the body louse (lice that live on the human body). Once doctors understood that lice were the cause of the infection, they knew what to fight. The biggest change? Hygiene.

Doctors proclaimed the benefits of soaps and bathing. Before people were admitted to the hospital, they were stripped of their clothing, shaved, and washed. This removed the lice from their bodies and prevented the spread of the disease.

Although doctors now knew the reason behind typhus, it was still hard to control. Soldiers in both World

War I and World War II suffered from attacks of typhus. The crowded conditions of tents and trenches provided a great breeding ground for lice.

Scientific advances during WWII brought about the invention of chemical insecticides and antibiotics. Today, typhus still exists in Central Africa, South America, and Asia, but epidemics are not frequent. Good hygiene, soap, clean public water systems, and antibiotics make typhus a rare guest, just like its host—the body louse.

CHAMPOO!

Hair washing was not popular in Europe in the Middle Ages. Bathing as a whole was discouraged because it was believed to be unhealthy. People thought that warm water opened up the pores of the skin and allowed disease to enter the body. A nice coating of dirt kept disease away from the skin and was much healthier than a bath. Most people just washed their hands, faces, and private parts.

Wealthy people rubbed their bodies with scented rags and perfumes. Men wore small bags stuffed with fragrant herbs tucked in their waistcoats and women used scented powders.

~continues on page 68~

CHAMPOOI

~continued from page 67~

But during the Middle Ages, countries in the Middle East were having a renaissance. Their physicians developed hospitals and teaching universities. They had spas and baths where people enjoyed massages, clean water, soap, and hair washing.

It wasn't until the 1800s that Europeans began to change their minds about the evils of bathing, with the help of a man from Bengali. Sake Dean Mahomed introduced champooi, or shampooing, and vapor massage when he opened a bath in Brighton, England. He advertised bathing as a cure when "everything else fails." Mahomed claimed that his baths and treatments would cure rheumatic and paralytic gout, stiff joints, old sprains, lame legs, and aches and pains.

The spa was an immediate success. The British decided they liked being clean and smelling nice. And they liked having scalps that weren't infested with lice.

ST. ANTHONY'S FIRE

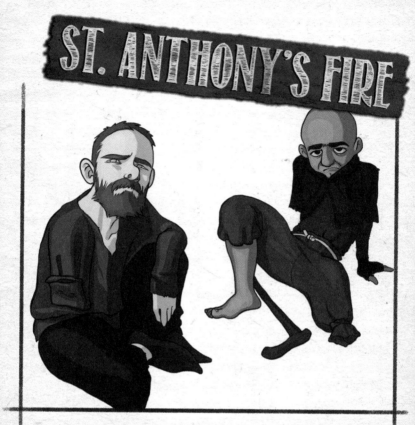

T he dirt road was filled with sick French trav-
elers. Some limped along on crutches, their
feet wrapped in rags, toes missing and fingers a horrible black color. Some were howl-
ing and twisting in a strange dance while their loved
ones tried to make them stay on the road. People
too sick to walk were carried on stretchers by family
or friends. They were all headed to the same place—
to see the monks at the Order of Hospitallers of St.
Anthony. It was their last and only hope.

The people were suffering from a strange disease that caused a horrible burning sensation in their arms and legs. Some people had seizures that caused them to jerk, hop, and scream in a wild dance that they could not stop until they passed out from exhaustion.

> Some limped along on crutches, their feet wrapped in rags, toes missing and fingers a horrible black color. Some were howling and twisting in a strange dance while their loved ones tried to make them stay on the road.

Nobody knew what caused the horrible disease, but they knew if they didn't get help they would die.

The monks gave their patients a very simple treatment. They cleaned their wounds, gave them rest, and fed them clean, wholesome meals. That simple treatment seemed to work a miracle. Patients improved. They stopped having seizures, their arms and legs stopped burning, and they became well enough to return home.

But once they went home, they became sick again. The seizures came back, they had hallucinations, and their arms and legs burned with pain. Fingers and toes became blackened and mummified, then fell off at the joint. The people desperately tried to get back to the monks. Many did not make it.

The people called it St. Anthony's Fire and believed it was a curse from God. The only thing that seemed to help was visiting one of the many French hospitals the monks had built. The horrible disease seemed to come and go. Some years it would affect hundreds of people in the French countryside. Other years, the people were spared the disease and could live in peace. From 870 AD to the 1600s, people in Europe suffered from the strange sickness.

It wasn't until 1670 that a French physician, Dr. Thuillier, began to suspect that the strange sickness was caused by something the people were eating. He examined the rye crop and the grain that was used to make rye bread. He noticed that in years when the disease was bad, there was a fungus that grew on the rye plant. He suspected it was this fungus that was making people sick, but the farmers didn't believe him. They ignored his warnings.

It took until 1853 for scientist Louis René Tulasne to prove that rye infected with the fungus was the cause of St. Anthony's Fire. The monks at the hospi-

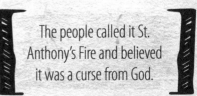

The people called it St. Anthony's Fire and believed it was a curse from God.

tals had provided the correct cure. They had served their patients clean food and had not made bread from the infected rye.

Modern scientists call the disease *ergotism* and know that it is caused by eating poisonous alkaloids in the rye fungus. There are two types of ergot poisoning. The first is convulsive ergotism and causes the seizures, hallucinations, and vomiting. The second type is gangrenous ergotism and kills the tissue in the fingers, hands, toes, and feet. The limbs die and fall off at the joint.

The best cure for the disease is prevention. Farmers and scientist have developed ways to monitor for the rye fungus, and in most modern countries, it is prevented from getting into the food supply. Ergotism does still happen in some developing nations where the fungus is not monitored as closely.

FREAKY FACT
SICK WITCHES?

It is entirely possible that the Salem Witch Trials of the 1600s were caused by ergotism, or eating infected rye. Scientists have found that in some types of ergotism, the rye fungus acts as a hallucinogen similar to LSD. The young girls at Salem who claimed to see visions and had convulsions may have been suffering from ergotism.

During that time period, many illnesses, accidents, and problems were blamed on the devil and his helpers. It would have been easy for the townspeople to think the girls' strange behavior was caused by witchcraft rather than by illness—although research is not conclusive, many historians believe that this is a possible explanation for the trials and convictions.

SWEATING SICKNESS

The ladies of King Henry VIII's court were enjoying a lovely summer luncheon when one of the women began shivering violently. The young woman was shaking as if she was naked in a snowstorm, but she was wearing the heavy dress of Tudor England and it was a very warm day. All the other women were fanning away the flies and heat.

Two other ladies-in-waiting escorted the sick girl back to her room and put her to bed. Once she was in bed, the girl complained of a head-ache and began sweating. By supper, she was dead.

The next morning, several more ladies and some of the men of the court were either shivering or sweating. The royal physician was called in. He knew exactly what was happening. The deadly sweating sickness had returned. He also knew there was nothing he could do to stop it. It was a disease like no other. People could wake up feeling fine and by suppertime, they were dead.

The physician had seen the disease before, but it had been more than 10 years prior. He knew that hundreds, perhaps thousands of people would die.

He had to protect the king, and the only thing he could recommend was quarantine.

Henry VIII was happy to comply. He was terrified of the sweating sickness and quickly left the court to go to a country home 12 miles away. He changed residences every few days so that he could avoid contact with anyone who might have been exposed to the terrible disease. The quarantine worked. King Henry VIII never fell ill, but more than half of his court fell sick and many died.

> Once she was in bed, the girl complained of a headache and began sweating. By supper, she was dead.

The sweating sickness first appeared in the summer of 1485 during the reign of King Henry VII. At the end of that summer, after hundreds of people had died, the disease disappeared. People breathed a sigh of relief. And for several years, it seemed the sweating sickness was gone. But it came back during the summer of 1507 and again in 1517. In Oxford and Cambridge, almost half the population died.

Doctors had no idea what caused the disease, but they knew the symptoms. The victims all complained of being cold and having a headache. Some felt giddy and light-headed. After an hour, most of them were delirious and covered in a drenching sweat that soaked their clothes and blankets. Many of the victims were dead within a few hours of feeling ill. Healthy young men and women began dying of the sweating disease. Unlike most illnesses that seemed to kill children or the elderly, this disease was deadliest for healthy people ages 16–30. If a patient managed to survive for 24 hours, he or she usually lived.

The sickness was so fast that there didn't seem to be much that doctors could offer in the way of a cure. Some tried bleeding the patient with leeches or cutting a slit between the shoulders. Others tried herbs laced with molasses or different teas, but nothing worked.

When King Henry VIII returned to court, he found that nearly half of the people had died. The sweating sickness had spread throughout England and into Ireland and Scotland. It spread across the English Channel and on to the European continent, killing thousands of people. Then it disappeared again until the summer of 1551 and once more in the summer of 1578. After that, the disease seems to vanish from history.

Modern doctors have been trying to solve the puzzle of the sweating sickness. They have researched all historical accounts and tried to match symptoms with other known diseases. Scientists know that it was not plague or typhus because the victims did not have the boils that come with plague or the rash of typhus.

When King Henry VIII returned to court, he found that nearly half of the people had died.

Scientists made a breakthrough in their research when they compared the symptoms to a modern disease—hantavirus. There was an outbreak of this illness in the summer of 1993 in the American Southwest. The victims all had a headache in the morning, then began sweating and had trouble breathing. By bedtime, they were in the hospital on respirators. The hantavirus also strikes young healthy adults. Scientists are almost certain that this may be the sweating sickness. To be sure, they need to dig up the grave of someone who was known to have died of the sweating sickness and see if they can get a sample of the virus from the dead body. That is not easily done because without living host tissue the virus will die and over many years there will be no evidence left.

But if it is the hantavirus, that would also answer the question as to why it only happened every few years. The hantavirus is carried on small rodents like deer mice that live in rural areas. They do not venture into cities or towns unless there is a food shortage. In summers with severe drought or floods, the mice will seek food sources in populated areas.

Someday, scientists may be able to know for certain what caused the sweating sickness, and if it appears again, they will be equipped with the right medicine to fight off a new epidemic.

A ROYAL PAIN IN THE REAR

King Louis XIV was one of the most power-ful rulers in French history. He commanded vast armies and built the grand Palace of Versailles. He also had a big problem with his rear end. A very big problem.

The growth on the king's rear was called an *anal fistula* and is a large painful swelling of blood vessels and tissue. It was so bad that it was difficult for the king to ride his horse or even sit on his throne. Nobody except the king's physicians knew about the huge mass growing on the king's backside. If anybody knew the king was sick or unwell, it could have caused panic, assassination attempts, or even war.

Every morning, physicians would check the king's health and record the growth of the fistula. They tried using herbal ointments and poultices to bring down the swelling, but they didn't help. The doctors thought enemas (cleaning the anus cavity with water and solutions) might help. They gave the king lots and lots of enemas. That didn't work.

> The growth on the king's rear was called an *anal fistula* and is a large painful swelling of blood vessels and tissue.

After more than a year of treatments, the physicians had to admit that nothing they were doing was helping and the fistula was getting larger. They feared the king could die from infection. The physicians had only one choice. They had to call in a surgeon.

During the 1600s, surgeons were considered much lower class than physicians. The Catholic Church warned against cutting into the human body, and physicians never performed any surgery. Besides, surgery was extremely dangerous. There was no safe anesthetic, so patients were usually awake during surgery. There were no antibiotics and no understanding of how to stop the bleeding. The majority of people who underwent surgery died. Surgery was only considered when there was no alternative and it was apparent that the patient was going to die.

The king's physicians knew that surgery was the only hope, but it was very risky. They called in the royal surgeon, Charles-François Félix, and asked him to operate on the king's rear.

Félix was not a stupid man. He realized that this was not only life or death for the king; it was life or death for him, too. If the king died during surgery, Félix would be blamed for killing the king, and he would certainly be executed. If he was successful, Félix would be rewarded with money, land, and a title. He would be rich and famous. Félix decided to take the risk, but he asked for 6 months to perfect his technique.

During the next 6 months, King Louis XIV's physicians tried to keep him as comfortable as possible, giving him enemas and

THE RETRACTOR

coating his rear with herbal ointments. Meanwhile, Félix
began his experiments.
He designed and
developed a special
scalpel and retrac-
tor and practiced
on more than 75
people. His practice
patients were either
convicted felons from
the local prison or patients
from the poorhouses. Some of his patients
lived and some of them died. When he had perfected his technique enough that the majority of his
patients lived, Félix was ready for surgery.

THE
"ROYALLY CURVED"
SCALPEL

On November 18, 1668, Félix was ready to operate on the Royal Rear of King Louis XIV. The royal
physicians, the Minister of State, and the king's son
were all gathered at the king's bedside to observe the
operation. Félix inserted the retractor and worked
with his special scalpel until he had removed the
huge fistula and bandaged the king's bottom. The
king was awake for the whole surgery.

To Félix and the king's relief, the surgery was a
success. The king was sitting up in bed in a month

On November 18, 1668, Félix was ready to operate on the Royal Rear of King Louis XIV. The royal physicians, the Minister of State, and the king's son were all gathered at the king's bedside to observe the operation.

and back riding his horse in 3 months. Félix was given the title Charles-François Félix de Tassy. He was awarded an estate and a huge sum of money.

Félix took the money and retired to his estate. He never picked up a scalpel again, even though he became famous in the French Court.

Once word got out about the king's surgery, it became all the rage in the court for people to wear bandages on their bottoms just like the king—even if they didn't have any medical problem. Surgery was elevated in esteem and more people were willing to consult with surgeons about their problems. Félix and his surgical skills had changed medicine. The king attended and encouraged others to attend public displays of surgery, and eventually the royal family supported the opening of the French Royal Academy of Surgery. And it all began with a pain in the royal rear end.

Medical Practice

MAKE FAKE SNOT

When you're sick, your head is often filled with snot. You blow out great green globs of the stuff and sometimes even cough it up. What the heck is that stuff anyway?

Another name for snot is mucus. There are mucus-producing tissues in the mouth, nose, sinuses, throat, lungs, and intestinal tract. Mucus acts as a protective blanket to keep these surfaces moist. When we get sick, these mucous membranes get irritated and produce lots more mucus or snot.

You can make fake snot with a few simple ingredients.

MATERIALS

- » Measuring cups
- » A bowl
- » A teaspoon
- » A fork
- » Boiling water (get an adult to help)
- » Gelatin (green or yellow is best)
- » Corn syrup

Fill the bowl with half a cup of boiling water. Add three teaspoons of gelatin to the bowl and stir with a fork. Add a quarter of a cup of corn syrup. Stir the mixture and look at the long strands of solution that have formed. These are like the strings of mucus in your body. Mucus is made from sugars and proteins (although different ones than in this recipe). The proteins and sugars make snot sticky and capable of stretching.

Now enjoy showing your fake snot to your friends.

Medical Practice

BREEDING BACTERIA

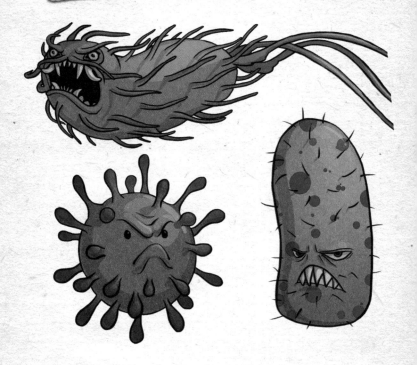

Doctors have been fighting bacteria since the world began. One of the reasons bacteria is so hard to get rid of is because it grows so fast. Grow your own crop of bacteria and see how quickly it reproduces.

MATERIALS

- » One packet of unfla- vored gelatin
- » Mixing bowl
- » Five small jar with lids
- » Two cups hot water
- » Cotton string
- » Masking tape
- » Marker
- » Magnifying glass

First, sterilize the jars and lids in a dishwasher or in a pot of boiling water.

When the jars and lids are cooled and ready to go, you need to prepare your growing solution.

Put the two cups of hot water in the mixing bowl and add the unflavored gelatin. Mix until dissolved. Pour the gelatin mix into each jar. Make sure to give each jar the same amount. Place a lid on one of the jars and use a marker and masking tape to label it "Control." (A control serves as a standard of comparison in any science experiment. By being sterile, it'll let you compare changes happening in your other jars.)

Cut four pieces of string (each about 5 inches long), and dip each string into the gelatin.

Now comes the fun part. You're going on a bacteria hunt. Find four different places in your house where you think there might be bacteria (such as on leftover food, in the trash can, in the fish tank, on your feet, in the bathroom sink). Get creative!

Rub each gelatin-soaked string in only one place.

Then place each string into the gelatin in separate jars. Label each jar with the place you rubbed the string. Then place lids on all of the jars.

Wait a week and see what grows in the jars.

Use your magnifying glass to look at the germs and bacteria you have grown. Do you see why it was hard for doctors to fight bacteria without strong medicine?

MODERN MARVELS

FATHER OF ANATOMY

Andreas Vesalius had an unusual hobby—he loved dissecting small animals. Dead squirrels and rabbits were his favorite treasures. While most young boys of the 1500s liked to play in the woods and hunt small game for food, Vesalius never gave his trophies to the family cook. Instead he took them home and cut them apart, examining the muscles, joints, and ligaments of each leg and arm. He cut into the abdomen and pulled out the liver, heart, and intestines. Then he cleaned the bones and reconstructed the skeletons. By the time he was a teenager, Vesalius was an expert at all kinds of dissection.

Growing up in family of doctors and pharmacists who encouraged his strange hobby, Vesalius was given medical books that diagrammed human and animal anatomies. He pored over the texts, and in 1533, at the age of 19, he enrolled at the University of Paris.

At university, Vesalius was shocked to learn the students did not learn anatomy through hands-on dissection of human bodies. Instead they were taught from an ancient Greek text that had been written by Aelius Galenus in the second century

> He cut into the stomach and pulled out the liver, heart, and intestines. Then he cleaned the bones and reconstructed the skeletons.

(200 AD). Once a year, the professors would perform a public dissection to show the students what the inside of a human body looked like. One professor would read from the ancient text while his assistant would hold up the body parts. Vesalius was horrified. How could anyone actually learn the parts of the human body without actual dissection?

How could they make any new discoveries?

Because Vesalius already had experience in dissection, he began working with the professors who did handle the rare cadavers. Vesalius soon began to realize that the ancient text the professors were

THE LADY CORPSE

Because it was rare for women to be hanged or beheaded, Vesalius's students had never worked on a female body. When they heard about a woman who had recently died, the students snuck into the graveyard and stole her body. But before they took it to Vesalius, they removed all of her skin so that she couldn't be identified.

Vesalius accepted the skinned body and taught the students about the human anatomy. A few days later, the woman's relatives accused Vesalius of stealing her body and experimenting on her. But since the students had skinned the body, there was no way for them to prove who it was. It would be centuries before the discovery of DNA.

using had serious mistakes. Pictures and descriptions of the human body in the text did not match what Vesalius was seeing in actual human bodies. He was sure that medical students were learning incorrect information because they were not actually dissecting the bodies.

Vesalius was right. Because the ancient church had banned dissection, the text was actually showing the body parts of pigs and apes. For centuries, no one had questioned the information because they had not done in-depth dissections.

> He was sure that medical students were learning incorrect information because they were not actually dissecting the bodies.

In the 1500s, the Catholic Church still frowned on human dissection, but they did allow Vesalius and his students to use the bodies of people who had been hung or beheaded for their crimes. Vesalius began giving public demonstrations of human anatomy and dissection. He had crowds of up to 500 people learning about the heart, stomach, muscles, and other organs of the body.

In 1543, at the age of 29, Vesalius published a new definitive work on the human body. He included more than 200 hand-drawn pictures of the human body. This work revolutionized medicine and the teaching of medical students. Vesalius became known as the founder of the modern study of anatomy.

THE BODY SNATCHERS

Under cover of darkness, the grave robbers frantically dug in the cemetery. They listened for the sound of footsteps or anything passing by. They weren't afraid of ghosts; they were afraid of the police. As soon as the shovel hit something solid, the men jumped into the hole and examined the coffin. They were lucky. It was only made of wood. Easy to pry open and pull out the body. Some of the richer folks were using metal coffins, and they were hard to break open.

Once the lid was open, they looked at their prize. The body didn't smell too bad. That was good. The fresher the body, the more money they could get.

The robbers hoisted the body into a bag and quickly left. They were anxious to sell the body and get rid of the evidence. They loaded the body into the back of a wagon and headed directly to the medical school. Tomorrow, the student doctors would have a new body to dissect.

> As soon as the shovel hit something solid, the men jumped into the hole and examined the coffin. They were lucky.

Body snatching was an illegal business in the 1800s, but it was one of the ways medical schools obtained cadavers for their students to study. Refrigeration had not been invented and there was no good way to preserve a body for the practicing students, so medical schools often pretended not to really know where their cadavers came from. It was a thriving business until some robbers decided it would be easier to kill people and bring in even fresher bodies. This resulted in the passage of the Anatomy Act of 1832 so that people could legally donate their bodies for medical study. It also made walking the streets of London much safer.

COFFIN COLLARS & COFFIN TORPEDOES

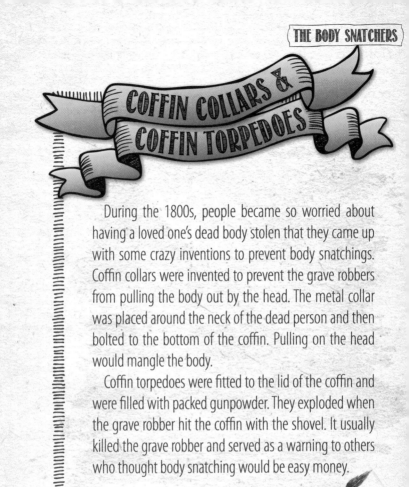

During the 1800s, people became so worried about having a loved one's dead body stolen that they came up with some crazy inventions to prevent body snatchings. Coffin collars were invented to prevent the grave robbers from pulling the body out by the head. The metal collar was placed around the neck of the dead person and then bolted to the bottom of the coffin. Pulling on the head would mangle the body.

Coffin torpedoes were fitted to the lid of the coffin and were filled with packed gunpowder. They exploded when the grave robber hit the coffin with the shovel. It usually killed the grave robber and served as a warning to others who thought body snatching would be easy money.

MINI MONSTERS

Recipe for Scorpions
Take a brick and carve an indentation. Then fill the hole with basil. Cover that brick with another one and set it in the sun. In just a few days, the basil will turn into scorpions.

Recipe for Bees
Slaughter a healthy bull and leave the body in the sun for several days. When the air and sun mix in the dead bull, it will create a swarm of bees that will fly out of the carcass.

The recipes sound like something from a witch's book of magic, but they were considered to be scientific fact before the invention of the microscope. For hundreds of years, people believed worms were created from mud, honeybees grew in flowers, and small fish were created in waves and sea foam. It was believed that both eels and frogs grew spontaneously from mud, and toads could be created from a dead duck placed on a pile of poop. Sickness and disease were caused by bad-smelling air, especially the stinky air from sewers and cesspools.

Sounds crazy, but without microscopes, people could not see the tiny eggs laid by invertebrate animals, so they believed the animals were created out of air, meat, or plants. This theory was called *spontaneous generation* and had some pretty important teachers and scientists who believed in the idea. Ancient Greek philosophers like Aristotle and Herodotus firmly believed that tiny animals just magically appeared in flower buds or rotten meat. They also thought that if they had the right recipe they could create these animals.

> It was believed that both eels and frogs grew spontaneously from mud, and toads could be created from a dead duck placed on a pile of poop.

Leave out rotting meat, and you magically get maggots and flies. It wasn't until the invention of the microscope that people were aware that there

Cells from Hooke's cork

were tiny particles in the world that were too small for the human eye to see, and some of those things were insect eggs.

Robert Hooke was one of the first people to make detailed drawings of what he saw with a microscope. In 1665, he published his drawings of lice, flies, feathers, and snowflakes in a book called *Micrographia*. It became a bestseller and people around the world began talking about the amazing "unseen" world. Hooke invented the term *cells* to describe the structures he saw in a slice of cork and in other pieces of plant material.

Antonie van Leeuwenhoek was inspired by Hooke's book to create his own set of magnifying lenses to study the "unseen" world. He created more than 500 microscopes and perfected his craft until he made a lens that magnified more than 200 times what the naked eye could see. This was stronger than any microscope of its time.

Leeuwenhoek used his lenses to examine everything from river water to human spit and was amazed to find that there were tiny living organisms in the water. Even more amazing, there were tiny animals living in his spit!

He reported his findings to the Royal Society of London, and the scientists thought Leeuwenhoek was either crazy or making up stories. They couldn't believe that there were living organisms so tiny that they couldn't be seen with the eye.

But Leeuwenhoek didn't give up. He kept writing letters to the Royal Society and telling them about the strange diving creatures he saw living in white matter he collected from an old man's mouth. He told them about the spinning, swirling "animalcules" he saw swimming in pond water.

Leeuwenhoek used his lenses to examine everything from river water to human spit and was amazed to find that there were tiny living organisms in the water.

The Royal Society decided they had to learn if he was telling the truth and hired Robert Hooke to duplicate his experiments. Hooke was astonished when he used the higher power magnification and saw the tiny animals swimming in drops of rainwater and bits of spit. The discovery of these tiny monsters changed the understanding of the natural world. With microscopes, scientists could see the tiny eggs that flies laid in meat. They could see the eggs of bees and scorpions. They began to understand that small animals reproduced in ways similar to larger animals.

But it was more than 100 years before they understood that some of the mini monsters swimming in mucus, drinking water, and eating poop were actually what made people sick.

MICROGRAPHIA

You can see Robert Hooke's book *Micrographia* online at https://ceb.nlm.nih.gov/proj/ttp/flash/hooke/hooke.html

Turn the pages and look at the details of seeds, insects, and leaves that amazed people of the 17th century. It's information that modern society takes for granted, but it was amazing news in 1665.

Hooke's drawing of a gnat

SOAP SAVES

The young mother writhed in the bed, moaning and sweating from the fever. Her husband and children listened to her cries and waited for what they knew was to come: her death. It was childbed fever, and it was feared by everyone who lived before the 20th century.

Today, having a baby is a joyful occasion. Everyone is excited for the mother to go to the hospital and the new little baby to be born. But in the past, childbirth was considered a life-threatening process. Scientists estimate that from the 1400s to 1800s, 10% of pregnant women died in childbirth.

Everyone is excited for the mother to go to the hospital and the new little baby to be born. But in the past, childbirth was considered a life-threatening process.

One of the greatest killers was childbed fever. When this happened, the mother had successfully delivered the baby, but then she became ill with a high fever and terrible pains in her abdomen. The fever could last from 3–10 days and was almost always fatal. Midwives and doctors didn't know how to stop the fever or what caused it.

Stories of the fever made young women terrified of giving birth. They often prepared for the delivery of the baby by making sure that their family and friends knew of their final wishes. They prayed for a safe delivery and a living baby.

In the 1800s, medicine was rapidly advancing. Scientists were learning about microscopic germs and bacteria. They were learning details about human anatomy through autopsies of cadavers and practicing medicine in hospitals.

In 1846, Ignaz Semmelweis was an assistant in Vienna's famous teaching hospital where there were two clinics for delivering babies. One was staffed by men studying to become doctors, and the other was staffed by women who worked as midwives. The clinic staffed by the midwives had a much higher survival rate for mothers. Only 3% of the women admitted to the midwife clinic died, but nearly 25% of the women who went to the doctors' hospital died.

Mothers quickly learned that they wanted to be in the clinic with the midwives and begged not to be admitted to the doctors' clinic. Semmelweis was determined to discover why one clinic had more deaths.

He began to research everything about the two clinics. He looked at the procedures they used to care for their patients. He checked to see if one clinic was more crowded than the other, or if they had different tools, but he could find no real variances. The only thing that was different was that midwives worked in the successful clinic and doctors worked in the clinic with more deaths.

Then, in 1847, a tragedy struck. His good friend

Ignaz Semmelweis, 1860

Jakob Kolletschka was accidentally poked with a student's scalpel during the examination of a dead body. Jakob died from a fever that was strangely similar to childbed fever.

Semmelweis did an autopsy on his friend, finding that the pathology was indeed similar to the fever that killed women in the maternity wards. He proposed that childbed fever was a result of contamination of the pregnant women with cadaver materials.

The doctors often examined cadavers and then went right into the delivery room with the mothers and helped birth the babies. The midwives never had contact with cadavers and their patients rarely got the fever.

Semmelweis immediately required doctors to wash their hands after leaving the autopsy room

and before entering the maternity ward. The deaths of women in the doctors' clinic dropped by 90%. Within a few months of instituting the handwashing policy, the death rates on

The doctors often examined cadavers and then went right into the delivery room with the mothers and helped birth the babies.

the doctors' ward and the midwives' ward were the same. Semmelweis had shown that childbed fever was a disease that could be controlled by cleanliness.

But doctors at that time still did not understand that disease was caused by germs. Doctors believed that disease was caused by bad air or an imbalance of blood. They couldn't believe that handwashing had anything to do with childbed fever, and Semmelweis's studies were largely ignored.

It would be another 20 years before Joseph Lister proved to the world that surgery and medicine needed to be done in a sterile environment. If doctors had listened to Semmelweis, thousands of lives could have been saved with just the help of soap.

MOLDY CURE

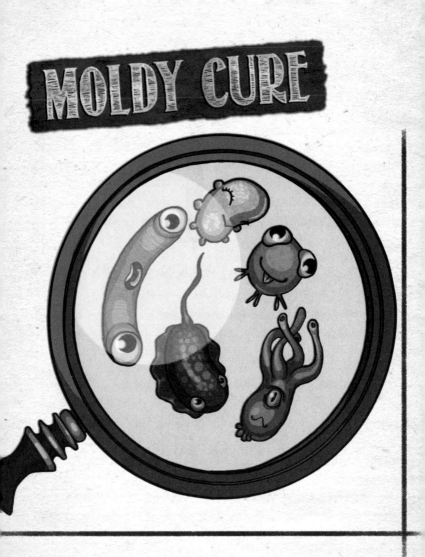

It was a cure as old as the pharaohs and samurai. To help cure a cut or pus-filled wound, plaster it with a piece of moldy bread. If early American settlers had sores or infected blisters, they covered them with a piece of moldy rye bread. And moldy cornbread was used to help cure the sores from measles.

But in the late 1800s and early 1900s, scientists and doctors discouraged people from using this "old time" cure. They were discovering vaccinations that could prevent rabies and antitoxins that helped with diphtheria and tetanus. They had discovered X-rays and vitamins. There was no need for people to cling to superstitious old cures like putting moldy bread on sores.

> To help cure a cut or pus-filled wound, plaster it with a piece of moldy bread. If early American settlers had sores or infected blisters, they covered them with a piece of moldy rye bread.

But then Alexander Fleming went on vacation in 1928 and made a discovery that changed the world. Fleming was a brilliant research scientist who had already discovered the enzyme lysozyme and was researching antibacterial agents that could be used to kill staphylococcus bacteria. Fleming was a great scientist, but he was a *lousy* housekeeper and was known for having a messy laboratory. When it was time for his family vacation, he stacked up a bunch of Petri dishes and left them in the corner of his laboratory bench.

When he came back a month later, he began cleaning up the pile of Petri dishes and noticed that one of the dishes was contaminated with a fungus. As he looked closer, he realized that the staphylococcus bacteria near the fungus had been killed. This was exactly what he had been researching. Could mold be the answer to stopping bacteria growth?

Fleming immediately went to work growing more of the mold in a pure culture. In experiments, he learned that the "mold juice," as he called it, could kill the bacteria that cause scarlet fever, pneumonia, meningitis, and diphtheria. It was an amazing discovery. Fleming named his mold juice *penicillin*.

It was the birth of modern antibiotics. Now diseases that had killed thousands were easily treated with simple pills. Pneumonia and meningitis patients survived their illnesses. Soldiers in WWII survived horrible wounds because penicillin prevented them from getting gangrene.

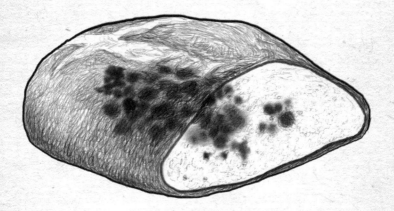

With the success of penicillin, scientists began researching other molds, plants, and natural substances to see what else might contain antibacterial properties. They discovered streptomycin, tetracycline, and other powerful antibiotics. Unfortunately, doctors did not understand that by using the antibiotics too much, bacteria would develop strains that are resistant to the antibiotics. Because of this, although antibiotics can fight serious illness, it is important that doctors and patients do not overuse them. Then, even strapping a piece of moldy bread to a wound won't do any good.

PANDEMIC

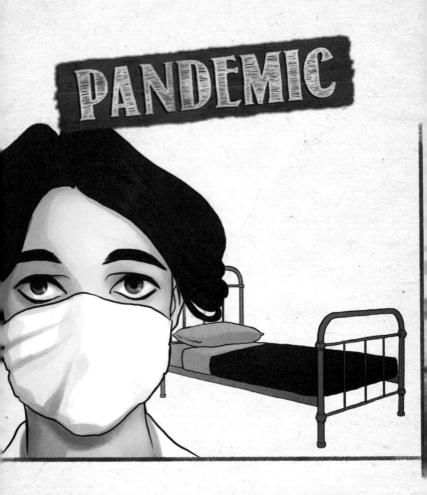

he first World War was still raging in Europe
during 1918, and everyone was frightened
that Germany would find a way to attack the
United States. So when people began dying
from the influenza virus, people were sure it was
germ warfare. Some people believed that the killer
influenza germs had been put into aspirin made
by the German drug company Bayer. People were

afraid to take an aspirin for a headache because they might die from influenza.

Other people thought that maybe one of the German U-boats had made it into Boston Harbor and released enough germs to infect the whole city. The Germans knew it would spread from Boston to all of America, and they would defeat the American Allies without having to shoot a single gun.

But what the Americans did not know was that the Germans had the same disease. The killer influenza was attacking just as many German citizens as American. The Germans were terrified that the Allies had attacked them with germ warfare in hope of killing soldiers and ending the war. Neither side wanted the other to know that their military was dying faster

Some people believed that the killer influenza germs had been put into aspirin made by the German drug company Bayer.

from influenza than from war wounds. They kept the news of the disease out of the papers and maintained a news blackout as much as they could. Neither side wanted the enemy to know about their weakness.

But people were dying at a rate that hadn't been seen since the plagues of the Middle Ages. Philadelphia was one of the hardest hit cities in America. In October of 1918, hundreds of people died each week. The dead were laid out on doorsteps at night so that they could be collected by horse-drawn wagons in the morning. So many people died that undertakers could not bury them individually and had to dig mass graves. Many people thought the world was coming to an end.

The disease spread quickly, sweeping from the East Coast to the Western United States. Cities were hit harder than rural areas, probably because the germs could be easily spread by coughing, sneezing, or from saliva and bodily fluids. People living in crowded cities spread the disease to each other.

But the United States wasn't the only place affected. The entire world—from India and Pakistan to Asia and Africa—saw millions of people die from influenza. And part of the reason that it became a worldwide epidemic was because of the war. As the troops sailed in ships from country to country, they spread the germs of influenza. The soldiers fighting the war were some of the hardest hit. Weakened by lack of food and months of living in trenches, the young men got sick and died quickly.

This strain of influenza was strange because it was most deadly to young, healthy adults. Usually children and the elderly were killed by the flu, but this time it was young teachers, mothers, fathers, shop clerks, nurses, doctors, and soldiers who were dying. In some families, all of the adults became ill and it was up to the children to nurse the parents.

Once a family member was diagnosed with influenza, the entire house was quarantined. They

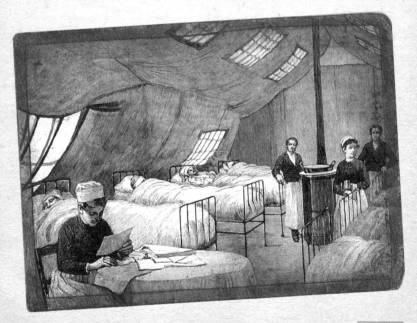

were not allowed to have contact with anyone outside their home. Without telephones, there was no way to call for help. Some children had both of their parents die, and millions around the world became orphans. More people died in the 1918 influenza pandemic than in the Black Plague or in the Great War.

Nobody knows the exact number of people who died because the newspapers did not report all the deaths for fear of creating more panic. A conservative estimate is that more than 50 million people died in 1918 from influenza.

> Once a family member was diagnosed with influenza, the entire house was quarantined. They were not allowed to have contact with anyone outside their home. Without telephones, there was no way to call for help.

One of the strangest parts of the epidemic is that it left just as fast as it came. By the time 1919 rolled around, the war was over and the epidemic had ended. Scientists are still trying to unravel the mystery of why this influenza strain was so deadly. They want to be prepared in case the virus ever infects humans again.

SALK TO THE RESCUE

It struck most often in the summer. Kids who were playing baseball one day were paralyzed the next. Some paralysis was so severe that children had to be placed in large metal machines just to keep them breathing. Nobody seemed to know what caused the disease or how to stop it. It was polio, and in the 1940s and 1950s, it paralyzed more than 500,000 people a year.

Scientists were confused. Polio seemed to come out of nowhere. Before the 1900s, no one knew about the disease. Health and sanitation conditions in America and Europe had greatly improved. Raw sewage didn't run in the streets anymore. There were modern sewers. People had indoor plumbing and flushing toilets. How could this be happening?

Every summer from 1916 onward, there was a polio epidemic in some part of the United States.

> Kids who were playing baseball one day were paralyzed the next. Some paralysis was so severe that children had to be placed in large metal machines just to keep them breathing.

When polio struck, doctors did what they could to stop the disease from spreading. The families of polio patients were quarantined. Official signs were placed on the front door and windows, warning the public that this house was a polio quarantine home and to stay away.

Cities closed their swimming pools and movie theaters. Parents warned children not to eat summer fruits like peaches or cherries for fear the germs were on the fruit. Children were kept inside and told not to play with friends. Summer vacation was not a carefree time of play—it was a time of worry and fear. Where would polio strike next and who would be paralyzed?

THE POLIO MYSTERY

So why did polio become a problem when the cities of America and Europe were getting cleaner? Doesn't disease happen when there is dirt, filth, and sewage everywhere?

The answer is complicated because polio is a disease that spreads through fecal matter (poop). In the old days when there was sewage in the streets, people were exposed to polio and most developed immunity to it. Some people did get sick, but there were also lots and lots of other diseases that people died from.

As health care improved and people used soap and got rid of garbage and human sewage in the streets, children were not exposed to the polio virus. They stopped building up immunity. So when the polio virus attacked, it became deadly or crippling. The only way to stop the disease was to build back the immunity through a vaccine.

Not everyone who got sick with polio became paralyzed or died. Some children only had a mild case and recovered quickly. But the fate of the paralyzed was so horrible that families were terrified. Many of the children spent the rest of their lives in wheelchairs or in heavy leg braces. Some spent months or years in a huge coffin-like machine called an *iron lung*. Only the head of the patient stuck out of the machine. It looked like some type of scientific torture device, but it used vacuum pressure to keep the patients' lungs breathing when the polio virus paralyzed them.

While parents tried everything they knew to keep their families safe from polio, scientists worked frantically on a cure. In 1935, a research scientist at New York University used ground-up monkey spinal cords that had been infected with the polio virus to develop a vaccine. He tried it on himself and several of his assistants first. When none of them got seriously ill, they tried the vaccine on 3,000 children. Lots of the kids had an allergic reaction to the vaccine, but none of them developed an immunity to polio.

It wasn't until 1952 that Jonas Salk created the first successful polio vaccine. And in 1954, the largest field test in history was launched with 1.8 million school children signing up to be polio pioneers. The vaccine was released to the public in 1955 and was declared safe and effective.

The rest of America quickly rolled up their sleeves and took the Salk cure. Polio cases dropped dramatically from 58,000 annual cases to just 5,600.

> And in 1954, the largest field test in history was launched with 1.8 million school children signing up to be polio pioneers.

The last case of paralytic polio in the United States occurred in 1979. Worldwide, polio decreased to only 359 cases reported in 2014. It is still a disease without a cure, but it can be prevented by the polio vaccine.

VERY BAD MEDICINE

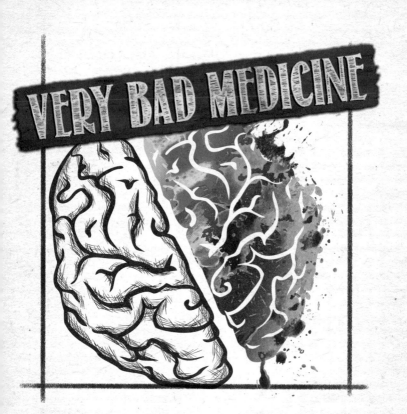

The brain is a mysterious organ. Scientists estimate a single brain contains 86 billion brain cells. Inside those billions of cells are 10,000 different neurons that process more than 50,000 thoughts a day. That's a lot of work going on in an organ that only weighs about 3 pounds.

Today, scientists know that the brain is critical for all functions of the body including movement, taste, intelligence, and even emotions. But in the 1800s, doctors were still learning about the brain and how it works. Brain surgery was very rare and often unsuccessful.

As a way to learn more about the brain and how it functioned, doctors often experimented on animals. In 1890, Friedrich Goltz was researching the brains of dogs. He did surgery on several dogs and removed a small portion of their temporal lobes. He observed that the dogs' personalities changed and they became calmer and less aggressive.

> Scientists estimate a single brain contains 86 billion brain cells. Inside those billions of cells are 10,000 different neurons that process more than 50,000 thoughts a day.

When Swiss doctor Gottlieb Burckhardt read about the experiments, he made the horrible decision to try this surgery on some of his patients who were suffering from schizophrenia (mental illness). Burckhardt thought that maybe removing part of their brains would make them calmer. Some of his six patients were calmer after the surgery, but two of them died.

The idea that mental illness could be cured by surgery was popular until the 1960s. This surgery was often referred to as a *lobotomy*. Some doctors drilled two holes in the skull and then cut the connecting tissue between the frontal lobe and the rest of the brain. Although this was dangerous to the patient, at least it was done in an operating room with surgeons.

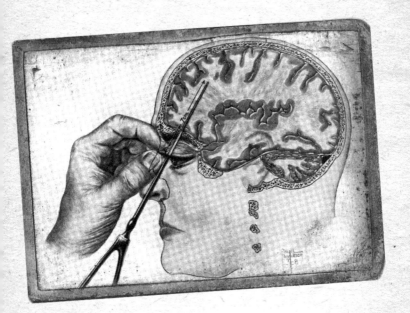

But in 1945, Dr. Walter Freeman began experimenting with a new way to do lobotomies. He wanted to find a way to do the operation in a doctor's office so that it would be less expensive and could be done on the patients in mental institutions.

Freeman used an ice pick from his own kitchen and began experimenting on grapefruit and then cadavers. He eventually developed a technique where he would drive the ice pick into the space between the eye socket and nose bone. The pick would go into the brain and be twisted to cut the connective tissue away from the frontal lobe of the brain.

Other surgeons were appalled by this method of operating on the brain, but many families were desperate to find a way to cure their loved ones of mental illness. Dr. Freeman performed his ice pick procedure on thousands of patients. Some of the patients were calmer and less agitated, but many of them lost their ability to think and reason normally. Several of the patients died, but Freeman

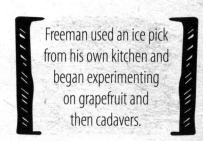

Freeman used an ice pick from his own kitchen and began experimenting on grapefruit and then cadavers.

made sure that newspapers wrote about the successful surgeries. It wasn't until the 1960s, when psychotropic drugs were invented, that lobotomies came to an end.

Today, doctors understand that mental illness is like any other sickness that can be treated with medicine and therapy. The days of ice pick lobotomies are long over.

THE STRANGE CASE OF
PHINEAS GAGE

In 1848, Phineas Gage was a hardworking young man. At the age of 25, he had the difficult job of a foreman of a railway construction team in Vermont. His supervisors trusted Gage with the most difficult tasks, including setting the explosives. Knowing how much blasting powder to use took brains and a steady hand. Gage had both.

But on September 13, something distracted Gage. He had just drilled a hole and filled it with powder. Then he used a large iron rod to carefully tamp down the powder. He had done so much work with blasting powder that he actually had a black-smith make a special tamping rod. It was shaped like a javelin with a tapered point at one end. It was more than a yard long.

Gage heard his men behind him and turned his head. At that moment, his tamping rod slipped and scraped against the hole, creating a spark. The blast that resulted launched the tamping rod point first through Gage's cheek, into his skull,

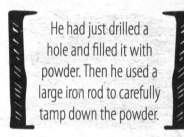

He had just drilled a hole and filled it with powder. Then he used a large iron rod to carefully tamp down the powder.

and out the other side. The rod landed almost 23 yards away, bloody and covered with Gage's brain tissue.

Gage's men rushed to his side, sure they would find him dead. Instead Gage was not only alive, but also able to stand up and talk to the men. He climbed into an ox cart and one of his friends drove him into town to be seen by a doctor. When the doc-

Phineas P. Gage with the actual tamping iron

tor arrived, Gage joked with him and said, "Here's business enough for you."

Dr. John Harlow was the man Gage joked with. Harlow cleaned Gage's wounds and worked for weeks to drain the infection. By January, Gage was physically much better, but it seems his personality had changed. His friends said that Gage had always been hardworking, responsible, and polite. Now he was unreliable, argumentative, and loved to swear. His friends said he was "no longer Gage." Unable to hold a job, Gage went home to recuperate with his family.

This was one of the first cases doctors had ever seen of someone who survived a traumatic brain injury and had a distinct personality change. After some months of recovery with his family, he was asked to visit medical schools so that doctors could study his case. Gage complied with the requests for a while, but eventually wanted to try to resume a more normal life.

Eventually, he worked at a stable in New Hampshire caring for horses, and later spent several years driving stagecoaches in Valparaíso, Chile. But 9 years after his accident, his health began to fail. He left Chile and moved to California where his family lived. Over the next few months, he had a series of seizures and died in 1860.

After Gage's death, his family donated his skull and tamping rod to the Warren Anatomical Museum at Harvard Medical School, where they are still on display today as one of the medical marvels of the 1800s.

> This was one of the first cases doctors had ever seen of someone who survived a traumatic brain injury and had a distinct personality change.

Today researchers are still interested in the story of Phineas Gage. Physicians credit Dr. Harlow with amazing skill at being able to keep Gage alive in a time without antibiotics or knowledge of modern brain surgery. His survival is indeed miraculous, but researchers are still trying to piece together the truth about what happened to his personality.

Immediately after the injury, he seemed to have a total personality change, but later reports appear to show a calmer tempered person who was able to hold a job. Obviously, he did suffer some brain damage, but without modern tools like MRIs and CAT scans (both invented in the 1970s), there is no real way to know the whole story.

Medical Practice

FEVER FIGHTER

A few centuries ago, physicians tried everything they could to lower a person's fever. They tried bloodletting, forced vomiting, eating cobwebs, and sleeping with onions in their socks. What doctors didn't understand was that the skin is the largest organ in the body. It has many functions and one of them is to control the temperature of the body. By cooling off the skin, it will help reduce a fever.

You can test it out yourself.

MATERIALS

- » Rubbing alcohol
- » Water
- » Two cotton balls
- » Two small plastic

cups
- » At least one partner
- » Blindfold
- » Paper and pencil

Pour a small amount of rubbing alcohol in one cup and water in the other cup. Blindfold your partners. Tell them you are going to touch their skin with two liquids and they should tell you which one feels cooler.

Have your partners hold out their wrists. Dab one wrist with the alcohol and one with the water. Have your partners report which one feels cooler. Try this again with different partners. Be sure to record your observations. You should find that people report the alcohol to feel cooler than the water. This is because alcohol evaporates faster than water. The evaporation cools the skin. How would this information have been useful to doctors in the 1600s? Would it have changed their prescriptions?

Medical Practice

MAKE YOUR OWN SCAB

Scabs are kind of gross. The brown crusty gunk that covers a nasty cut or scrape isn't pretty, but it is very necessary. When the body gets a cut, scrape, or break in the skin, special blood cells called *platelets* form at the site. The platelets stick together like glue and form a clot that stops the bleeding. In the clot can also be found thread-like fibers called *fibrin*. They hold the clot together. The scab protects the body from infection entering the blood and skin.

You can see how scabs work with this experiment.

MATERIALS

- » Paper plate
- » Tiny pieces of brown and red paper (the size of confetti)
- » Brown or red paint
- » School glue
- » Table knife
- » Apple
- » Paintbrush

Before you begin, add a few drops of the red or brown paint to the glue and mix it together.

You are going to give the apple an injury just like a person gets a scrape on his or her skin. Use the table knife to scrape away some of the apple peel. Do this in two places on the apple. Make them small scrapes. Don't skin the whole apple!

Next, you are going to make a scab to cover one of the scrapes on the apple. The other scrape will be left uncovered. Paint the apple scrape with the colored glue. This represents the fibrin. Next, sprinkle the paper confetti on the glue. This represents the platelets. Repeat this one more time so you have a nice thick scab. Then set your apple on the paper plate and let the scab dry. Wait 24 hours and then remove the scab. Compare the two apple scrapes. What difference did the scab make? How important is a scab on human skin?

BIBLIOGRAPHY

BOOKS

Barry, J. M. (2005). *The great influenza: The story of the deadliest pandemic in history* (Rev. ed.). New York, NY: Penguin.

Belofsky, N. (2013). *Strange medicine: A shocking history of real medical practices through the ages.* New York, NY: Perigee.

Davies, P. (2000). *The devil's flu: The world's deadliest influenza epidemic and the scientific hunt for the virus that caused it.* New York, NY: Henry Holt.

Dobson, M. (2007). *Disease: The story of disease and mankind's continuing struggle against it.* London, England: Quercus.

Dobson, M. (2013). *The story of medicine: From bloodletting to biotechnology.* London, England: Quercus.

Harrison, I. (2004). *The book of inventions.* Washington, DC: National Geographic.

Jardine, L. (2005). *The curious life of Robert Hooke.* New York, NY: Harper Collins.

Kolata, G. (2001). *Flu: The story of the great influenza pandemic of 1918 and the search for the virus that caused it.* New York, NY: Touchstone.

Parker, S. (2013). *Kill or cure: An illustrated history of medicine.* London, England: DK.

WEBSITES

American Chemical Society. (2016). *Discovery and development of penicillin.* Retrieved from http://www.acs.org/content/acs/en/education/whatischemistry/landmarks/flemingpenicillin.html

Ancient Egyptian medicine. (2000). Retrieved from http://www.reshafim.org.il/ad/egypt/timelines/topics/medicine.htm

The Anne Boleyn Files. (n.d.). *What was sweating sickness?* Retrieved from http://www.theanne boleynfiles.com/q-a/what-was-sweating-sick ness

BBC News. (2001). *Prehistoric dentistry evidence found.* Retrieved from http://news.bbc.co.uk/2/ hi/health/1272010.stm

Benedictow, O. J. (2005). The Black Death: The greatest catastrophe ever. *History Today, 55*(3). Retrieved from http://www.historytoday.com/ ole-j-benedictow/black-death-greatest-catas trophe-ever

Biography.com. (n.d.). *Louis XIV.* Retrieved from http://www.biography.com/people/louis-xiv-9386885

CBS News. (n.d.). *Polio vaccine: A look back.* Retrieved from http://www.cbsnews.com/pic tures/polio-vaccine-turns-58-a-look-back/7

Chateau Versailles. (n.d.). *Sciences & curiosities at the Court of Versailles: Scalpel and retractor.* Retrieved from http://sciences.chateau versailles.fr

Chen, L. (2014). The old and mysterious practice of eating dirt, revealed. *NPR.* Retrieved from http://www.npr.org/sections/thesalt/2014/

04/02/297881388/the-old-and-mysterious-practice-of-eating-dirt-revealed

Cohen, J. (2012). 9 bizarre baldness cures. *History.com*. Retrieved from http://www.history.com/news/history-lists/9-bizarre-baldness-cures

Davis, L. (2013). 8 ways to keep body snatchers from stealing your corpse. *io9*. Retrieved from http://io9.com/8-ways-to-keep-body-snatchers-from-stealing-your-corpse-1444488983

Discover Magazine. (1997). *The sweating sickness returns.* Retrieved from http://discovermagazine.com/1997/jun/thesweatingsickn1161

Dwight, C., Korthase, A. M., & Gonzales-Ralya, A. (1999). *The faces behind the masks: The "toilette" in 18th century England.* Retrieved from http://www.umich.edu/~ece/student_projects/leisure/sanitation.html

Gilbert, R. (n.d.). *Medieval hair care: Grooming tools, treatments, and colouring.* Retrieved from http://rosaliegilbert.com/haircare.html

Greenstone, G. (2010). The history of bloodletting. *BC Medical Journal, 52,* 12–14. Retrieved from http://www.bcmj.org/premise/history-bloodletting

Grossman, S. K. (2008). *Death by rye bread.* Retrieved from http://historybizarremysterious.

blogspot.com/2008/03/death-by-rye-bread.
html

History.com. (n.d.). *Black death.* Retrieved from
http://www.history.com/topics/black-death

Kantor, J. H. (2015). 10 ancient medical practices we
thankfully abandoned. *Listverse.* Retrieved from
http://listverse.com/2015/03/13/10-ancient-
medical-practices-we-thankfully-abandoned

Kean, S. (2014). How Phineas Gage survived a hor-
rific brain injury to become one of the most
famous names in medical history. *National Post.*
Retrieved from http://news.nationalpost.com/
news/how-phineas-gage-survived-a-horrific-
brain-injury-to-become-one-of-the-most-
famous-names-in-medical-history

Kelly, D. (2014). 10 disturbing stories about history's body snatchers. *Listverse.* Retrieved from
http://listverse.com/2014/10/13/10-disturbing-
stories-about-historys-body-snatchers

KQED. (2001). *Bloodletting: Barber surgeons and
early medicine: Early practitioners.* Retrieved
from http://www.pbs.org/kqed/demonbarber/
bloodletting

Lapinskas, V. (2007). A brief history of ergotism:
From St. Anthony's fire and St. Vitus' dance until
today. *Medicinos Istorija, 13,* 202–206. Retrieved

from http://www.mtp.lt/files/MEDICINA-2007-2-16-LAPIN.pdf

Levine, R., & Evers, C. (n.d.). The slow death of spontaneous generation (1668–1859). *National Health Museum*. Retrieved from http://web projects.oit.ncsu.edu/project/bio183de/Black/cellintro/cellintro_reading/Spontaneous_Generation.html

Lewith, G. T. (n.d.). *Acupuncture: The history of acupuncture in China*. Retrieved from http://www.healthy.net/Health/Article/The_History_of_Acupuncture_in_China/1819

Lingo, A. K. (n.d.). *Obstetrics and midwifery*. Retrieved from http://www.faqs.org/childhood/Me-Pa/Obstetrics-and-Midwifery.html

Littman, G. (2014). The royal fistula that changed the face of surgery. *Bilan*. Retrieved from http://www.bilan.ch/garry-littman/english-room/royal-fistula-changed-face-surgery

Medieval hygiene. (2011). Retrieved from https://rautakyy.wordpress.com/2011/01/05/medieval-hygiene

Meštrović, T. (2015). Smallpox history. *News Medical*. Retrieved from http://www.news-medical.net/health/Smallpox-History.aspx

Myers, G. (2014). 10 awful realities behind the lobotomy craze. *Listverse*. Retrieved from http://listverse.com/2014/11/20/10-awful-realities-behind-the-lobotomy-craze

Nix, E. (2014). Why are barber poles red, white and blue? *History.com*. Retrieved from http://www.history.com/news/ask-history/why-are-barber-poles-red-white-and-blue

Science Museum, London. (n.d.). *Barber-surgeons*. Retrieved from http://www.sciencemuseum.org.uk/broughttolife/people/barbersurgeons

Science Museum, London. (n.d.). *Leech collectors*. Retrieved from http://www.sciencemuseum.org.uk/broughttolife/people/leechcollectors

ScienceBlogs. (2007). *The rise & fall of the prefrontal lobotomy*. Retrieved from http://scienceblogs.com/neurophilosophy/2007/07/24/inventing-the-lobotomy

Starks, P. T. B., & Slabach, B. L. (2012). Would you like a side of dirt with that? *Scientific American*. Retrieved from http://www.scientificamerican.com/article/would-you-like-side-dirt-eating-soil

Swancer, B. (2015). The bizarre honey mummies of ancient Arabia. *Mysterious Universe*. Retrieved from http://mysteriousuniverse.org/2015/05/the-bizarre-honey-mummies-of-ancient-arabia

"Truth and myth" by Dr. Daniel H. Garrison. (n.d.). *Vesalius Fabrica.* Retrieved from http://www.vesaliusfabrica.com/en/vesalius/truth-and-myth/selected-stories.html

Twomey, S. (2010). Phineas Gage: Neuroscience's most famous patient. *Smithsonian Magazine.* Retrieved from http://www.smithsonianmag.com/history/phineas-gage-neurosciences-most-famous-patient-11390067

United States Department of Health and Human Services. (n.d.). *The great pandemic: The United States in 1918–1919.* Retrieved from http://www.flu.gov/pandemic/history/1918

Vogel, M. R. (n.d.). *Ergotism and Salem.* Retrieved from http://www.foodreference.com/html/a-ergotism-salem.html

Wikipedia. (n.d.). *1918 flu pandemic.* Retrieved from https://en.wikipedia.org/wiki/1918_flu_pandemic

Wikipedia. (n.d.). *Acupuncture.* Retrieved from https://en.wikipedia.org/wiki/Acupuncture

Wikipedia. (n.d.). *Bloodletting.* Retrieved from https://en.wikipedia.org/wiki/Bloodletting

Wikipedia. (n.d.). *Body snatching.* Retrieved from https://en.wikipedia.org/wiki/Body_snatching

Wikipedia. (n.d.). *Ergotism.* Retrieved from https://en.wikipedia.org/wiki/Ergotism

Wikipedia. (n.d.). *History of poliomyelitis.* Retrieved from https://en.wikipedia.org/wiki/History_of_poliomyelitis

Wikipedia. (n.d.). *History of smallpox.* Retrieved from https://en.wikipedia.org/wiki/History_of_smallpox

Wikipedia. (n.d.). *Ignaz Semmelweis.* Retrieved from https://en.wikipedia.org/wiki/Ignaz_Semmelweis

Wikipedia. (n.d.). *Iron lung.* Retrieved from https://en.wikipedia.org/wiki/Iron_lung

Wikipedia. (n.d.). *Medicine in the medieval Islamic world.* Retrieved from https://en.wikipedia.org/wiki/Medicine_in_the_medieval_Islamic_world

Wikipedia. (n.d.). *Mellified man.* Retrieved from https://en.wikipedia.org/wiki/Mellified_man

Wikipedia. (n.d.). *Plague doctor.* Retrieved from https://en.wikipedia.org/wiki/Plague_doctor

Wikipedia. (n.d.). *Sake Dean Mahomed.* Retrieved from https://en.wikipedia.org/wiki/Sake_Dean_Mahomed

Woywodt, A., & Kiss, A. (2002). Geophagia: The history of earth-eating. *Journal of the Royal Society of Medicine, 95,* 143–146. Retrieved from http://www.ncbi.nlm.nih.gov/pmc/articles/PMC1279487

Stephanie Bearce is a writer, teacher, and science nerd. She likes teaching kids how to blow up toothpaste and dissect worms. She also loves collecting rocks and keeps a huge collection of fossilized bones in her basement. When she is not exploding experiments in her kitchen or researching strange science facts in the library, Stephanie likes to explore catacombs and museums with her husband, Darrell.

MORE TWISTED TRUE TALES FROM SCIENCE

Twisted True Tales From Science: Disaster Discoveries

ISBN: 978-1-61821-574-1

London was once covered in a fog so polluted that it killed 12,000 people. The Aleppo earthquake killed 230,000 people, and a wall of water mysteriously wiped out the whole town of Burnam-on-the-Sea. All of these were catastrophic disasters, but they led to important discoveries in science. Learn about how the earth turned to liquid in New Zealand, and what happens when a tsunami meets a nuclear reactor. These stories may sound twisted and strange, but they are all true tales from science!

MORE TWISTED TRUE TALES FROM SCIENCE

Twisted True Tales From Science: Explosive Experiments

ISBN: 978-1-61821-576-5

Two thousand years ago Chinese scientists were looking for a medicine that would make them live forever. Instead, they blew up their lab and discovered gunpowder. Alfred Nobel blew up his laboratory twice before he discovered the formula for dynamite. Learn about the Apollo 13 and Challenger explosions, and the strange space explosions caused by top secret Starfish Prime. These stories may sound twisted, but they're all true tales from science!

MORE TWISTED TRUE TALES FROM SCIENCE

Twisted True Tales From Science: Insane Inventors

978-1-61821-570-3

Nikola Tesla was crazy smart. He invented the idea for cell phones in 1893, discovered alternating current, and invented a death ray gun. Of course, he also talked to pigeons, ate only boiled food, and was scared of women who wore jewelry. He was an insane inventor. So was Henry Cavendish, who discovered hydrogen, calculated the density of the Earth, and was so scared of people that he had to write notes to communicate. Sir Isaac Newton discovered the laws of gravity, believed in magic, and thought he could make a potion to create gold. These stories may sound twisted, but they're all true tales from science!